## Praise for Kynes' *Plant Magi*

"There are a great many gems to be discovered in this book, making it a terrific gift at any time of the year."

—Karen M. Rider for *Inner Tapestry*

"From beginner to advanced, this book can provide easy-to-use rituals, as well as a perspective that many experienced Pagans may not have thought of."

—Deirdre Hebert, hostess, *PaganFM!*

"If you need to find some sanity, then this book is ideal. You won't regret buying this book, especially if you need a spiritual rejuvenation."

—*Sydney Star Observer*, July 2008

"… full of wisdom and power."

—*The Rowdy Goddess Blog*

*Photo by Jessica Weiser*

## About the Author

Sandra Kynes is an explorer of history, myth, and magic. Although she is a member of the Order of Bards, Ovates and Druids, she travels a solitary Goddess-centered path through the Druidic woods. She likes to develop creative ways to explore the world and integrate them with her spiritual path, which serves as the basis for her books. Sandra has lived in New York City, Europe, and England. She now lives in coastal New England in a Victorian-era house with her family, cats, and a couple of ghosts. In addition to writing, she is a yoga instructor and Reiki practitioner. Sandra enjoys connecting with nature through gardening, hiking, bird watching, and ocean kayaking. Visit her website at www.kynes.net.

## Also by Sandra Kynes

*Bird Magic*

*Herb Gardener's Essential Guide*

*Star Magic*

*Mixing Essential Oils for Magic*

*Llewellyn's Complete Book of Correspondences*

*Change at Hand*

*Sea Magic*

*Your Altar*

*Whispers from the Woods*

*A Year of Ritual*

*Gemstone Feng Shui*

# Plant
# magic

A Year of Green Wisdom for Pagans & Wiccans

# SANDRA KYNES

Llewellyn Publications
Woodbury, Minnesota

FIRST EDITION
Second Printing, 2020

Book design by Bob Gaul
Chapter opening art by Wen Hsu
Cover design by Lisa Novak
Cover illustration by Chris Coccoza
Editing by Aaron Lawrence
Interior figures, oghams and runes by Llewellyn art department

Llewellyn Publications is a registered trademark of Llewellyn Worldwide Ltd.

**Library of Congress Cataloging-in-Publication Data**
The Library of Congress has already cataloged an earlier printing under LCCN: 2016054412

Llewellyn Worldwide Ltd. does not participate in, endorse, or have any authority or responsibility concerning private business transactions between our authors and the public.

All mail addressed to the author is forwarded, but the publisher cannot, unless specifically instructed by the author, give out an address or phone number.

Any Internet references contained in this work are current at publication time, but the publisher cannot guarantee that a specific location will continue to be maintained. Please refer to the publisher's website for links to authors' websites and other sources.

Llewellyn Publications
A Division of Llewellyn Worldwide Ltd.
2143 Wooddale Drive
Woodbury, MN 55125-2989
www.llewellyn.com

Printed in the United States of America

# Contents

# Introduction

The green world is enchanting and powerful, but unfortunately we spend so much time indoors and in cars that it's easy to lose contact with nature. This makes it difficult to develop and maintain a working knowledge of plants.

Throughout the ages, witchcraft was intimately linked with plants. The witches, wise women and men, were the ones village people went to for medicine and magic. In addition to knowing what to use, they knew when plants came into leaf, bloomed, and produced seed or fruit. These people lived with the seasons. While we have the luxury of buying what we want whenever we want, change is afoot in the mundane world with a movement that focuses on seasonal and local food. For Pagans and Wiccans, this goes hand-in-hand with a spiritual path that celebrates the seasonal wheel of the year.

The sabbats form the spokes of this wheel, and there are certain traditional plants used to mark these occasions. But what about the time in between these metaphorical spokes? Of course it's not devoid of plants because we use them for a range of magical purposes. However, the plants that we use don't always coincide with the cycle of the green world. Granted we can dry and store plants for later use as people have done for thousands of years, but how many of us know when to gather cinquefoil, sweet woodruff, or haws? Do we even know where to look for mullein?

Whether or not we garden or search the woods, the wisdom of plants comes alive when we work with them within the context of the seasons and learn how their cycles progress month by month. Basing our magical use of plants within the seasons also helps us develop more meaningful ways to connect with the green world and the realm of nature spirits. This, in turn, provides our rituals and magic with more continuity, creating a natural flow as we go through the year.

This book is a tool for learning about both ordinary and classically witchy plants. Going month by month, it highlights a range of plants from small herbs to mighty trees. Included are facts about the plant's physical characteristics, its history and folklore, and how it can be used magically. While this book focuses on North American plants, we will see how plant mythology and folklore was often carried here by European settlers and applied to similar plants. In many cases, settlers brought plants with them to the New World.

The first chapter, "Getting Started," provides information on connecting with the spirit and energy of plants, why scientific names are important, some frequently-used words that are good to know, and precautions about using and working with plants. We will also take a look at planetary and fixed star influences and, of course, the moon's effect on plants for lunar gardening. Last but not least, we will see how the symbolism of the various parts of plants can be utilized.

Each subsequent chapter focuses on a month and is divided into four sections. The first section is called "On the Calendar" and takes note of sabbats, Celtic tree months, and other significant dates that involve plants. The next two sections are called "In the Garden" and "In the Wild." These highlight plants that may be blooming or bearing fruit that month. As expected, these two sections are somewhat fluid as some wild plants have become popular in the garden and some garden plants have found homes outside of our backyards. The last section in each of these chapters is called "In the House." This section focuses on indoor, plant-related projects and activities, though there is occasional overlap with the previous two sections.

This book provides a look at what is generally considered classical seasonal change, which is most closely mirrored in the Mid-Atlantic and Midwestern states. Of course, there are regional variations. I live in northern New England and our seasons lag behind many other areas of the country. However, the progression of development and growth and the interrelationship of plants follow the same cycle. Keeping notes on how the seasons unfold in your area will give you a sense of continuity throughout the year. Keep a journal of where and when you find plants in bloom and when they come into seed or produce fruit. Understanding and working with plants through the seasons reveals nuances that personalize our experience with the green world and helps to build our knowledge base for magic.

This book is intended to inform and inspire you. Being familiar with nature's cycles connects us more closely with the green world and with all the wise folk who have gone before us as we carry on their work with plant magic. In addition, working with plants helps us grow as individuals and discover our unique ways of self-expression in the craft.

# Getting Started

When you decide to do more than reach for a jar of dried herbs on your kitchen shelf for magic, you are taking a big step into the enchanting world of plants. While the first few steps may seem intimidating—upon realizing the vastness and complexity of the green world—it is also exciting to know that you are joining the ranks of all those wise women and men of the past who worked with plants for magic.

## Why Scientific Names Are Important

While the common names for plants are easy to remember, they are a continual source of confusion because one plant may be known by a number of different names. For example, the plant commonly known as meadowsweet (*Filipendula ulmaria*) is also called queen of the meadow. And the plant commonly known as gravel root (*Eutrochium purpureum*) is also known as meadowsweet and queen of the meadow. For this reason, it is important to know the scientific (genus and species) names when studying or purchasing plants or plant material.

In addition, some names often get applied incorrectly, causing more confusion. For example, both northern adder's tongue (*Ophioglossum pusillum*) and American trout-lily (*Erythronium americanum*) are called adder's tongue. And while dogtooth violet is another name for the trout-lily, it has sometimes been applied to northern adder's tongue. This may seem like minor confusion on paper, but it is important to know which plants we are using because some are extremely toxic and can be dangerous to handle.

When working with plants in the wild, in addition to toxicity it is important to know whether or not a plant is considered endangered or threatened in your area. For example, all the trout lilies (from the genus *Erythronium*) are endangered in Florida. A good resource for information on endangered or threatened species is the US Department of Agriculture's website database at: http://plants.usda.gov/threat.html.

Don't be overwhelmed by so much information, just be aware and open to learning. Let's start by understanding scientific names. The genus and species of a plant are part of a complex naming structure initiated by Swedish naturalist, Carl Linnaeus (1707–1778). His work became the foundation for the International Code of Botanical Nomenclature.

While Table 1 illustrates the basic seven-level hierarchy of plant classification, the full modern taxonomy has at least sixteen levels, which includes super-divisions and orders, sub-classes and families, and more. For simplicity, we will deal mostly with genus and species with a few mentions of family.

| Table 1. The Basic Hierarchy of Plants |
| --- |
| Kingdom > Phylum/Division > Class > Order > Family > Genus > Species |

As new information about plants emerged over time, their names were changed to reflect the new data. This is one reason why we find synonyms in botanical names. For example, the scientific names for the belladonna lily are noted as *Amaryllis belladonna* syn. *Callicore rosea*. Synonyms are used because the antiquated names have been kept to aid in plant identification. Another reason is scientific disagreement.

Most names are in Latin because this was a common language that people who were engaged in scientific research used during Linnaeus's time. The first of the two words in the scientific name is the genus, which is a proper noun and always capitalized. A plant's species name is an adjective that usually provides a little description about the plant. The genus for yarrow is *Achillea* in honor of the Greek hero Achilles, and one species of yarrow is *millefolium*. The word *millefolium* indicates a leaf of many parts (*mille* meaning "thousands" and *folium*, "foliage").

Occasionally you may see a third word in a scientific name preceded with "var." This indicates that it is a variety of that species. For example, the white-flowered rosemary has the scientific name of *Rosmarinus officinalis* var. *albiflorus*. A variety is a naturally occurring variation in a species. On the other hand, a cultivar, or cultivated variety, is a variety that was created by human hands. Cultivar names are most often in English surrounded by single quotes. An example is a type of rose *Rosa floribunda* 'Angel Face.'

An "×" in a name indicates that the plant is a hybrid between two species. *Mentha × piperita*, peppermint, is a naturally occurring hybrid between spearmint, *Mentha spicata*, and water mint, *Mentha aquatica*.

While it is not necessary to memorize scientific names, write down the names for the plants you work with so you can always refer to them when necessary. This is important if you are purchasing plants or if you are working with their essential oils so you can be sure to get the correct ones. And, of course, it helps when checking if wild plants are endangered.

## Frequently Used Words and Terms to Know

As you go through the names of plants, some words appear often, such as the word "wort," as in Saint John's wort. This comes from the Old English *wyrt*, meaning "plant" or "herb."[1] Bane is another word that we find in wolfsbane, henbane, and others. This is an

---

1   Philip Durkin, *The Oxford Guide to Etymology* (New York: Oxford University Press, 2009), xxxviii.

Anglo-Saxon word for poison, and it was incorporated into the names of toxic plants as a warning.[2]

We also find some words frequently cropping up in scientific names. *Vulgaris*, as in thyme (*Thymus vulgaris*) or in primrose (*Primula vulgaris),* means "common." *Officinale* or *officinalis*, as in dandelion (*Taraxacum officinale*) or vervain (*Verbena officinalis*), means that it is (or was when the plant was named) officially recognized as a medicinal plant. *Anthe* in both the scientific and common name for the chrysanthemum comes from the Greek *anthos,* meaning "flower." The Latin *folia* and *folium* means "foliage," and we find it in the American beech (*Fagus grandifolia*), meaning "grand foliage," and, as mentioned, yarrow (*Achillea millefolium*), "thousand-leafed."

There are also some botanical terms that are helpful to know. Throughout the book, plants may be referred to as an annual, biennial, or perennial. As its name implies, an annual plant completes its life cycle in one year. It flowers, sets seed, and dies in a single growing season. German chamomile (*Matricaria recutita*) and the common sunflower (*Helianthus annuus*) are examples.

Biennials take two seasons. These usually only bloom and set seed in their second year. Angelica (*Angelica archangelica*) and mullein (*Verbascum thapsus*) are examples of biennials. Perennials live from year to year. Solomon's seal (*Polygonatum biflorum*) and lady's mantle (*Alchemilla vulgaris*) are examples of perennials. While the top portion of these plants die back in the autumn, the roots remain alive but dormant through winter. In the spring, perennials come up again. Table 2 provides a list of other helpful terms.

| Table 2. A Brief Listing of Helpful Botanical Terms | |
|---|---|
| Axil | The area of a plant between a stem or branch and a leaf stem |
| Basal leaves | Leaves at the base of an upright stem that are different from those on the stem |

---

2   Wolf D. Storl, *The Herbal Lore of Wise Women and Wortcunners: The Healing Power of Medicinal Plants* (Berkeley, CA: North Atlantic Books), 234, 2012.

| Table 2. A Brief Listing of Helpful Botanical Terms (continued) ||
|---|---|
| Catkin | A thick, usually drooping, cluster of tiny flowers |
| Flower head | A dense, compact cluster of tiny flowers |
| Lobed | A leaf with deeply indented edges, such as oak or maple tree leaves |
| Rhizome | An underground stem that is usually considered as a type of root |
| Sepal | The outermost part of a flower that protects the young bud and is usually green |
| Toothed | A leaf with jagged edges, also called serrated |
| Umbel | A flower head structure (think umbrella) that can be flat-topped or globe-shaped |
| Whorl | A circular or spiral growth pattern of leaves, needles, or flower petals |

## Precautions

Handling and using plants must be done with knowledge and common sense, and with safety in mind. Women who are pregnant or nursing must be especially careful. The banes, of course, are poisonous, but other common plants are poisonous or toxic, too. While some of these should not be handled, others can be done so with care. When in doubt identifying wild plants, it is best to avoid working with them.

## Astrological Influences

Since ancient times, the movement of the planets was used to determine the most appropriate time for various agricultural tasks. The Greek poet and farmer Hesiod (circa 650 BCE) advised others on how to use the planets and stars for determining the right time to plant and harvest their fields.

Up through the Middle Ages, astrology was closely integrated with astronomy, mathematics, and medicine. This extended to understanding the celestial influences on medicinal plants. The famed English herbalist Nicholas Culpeper (1616–1654) wrote several books on astrology and integrated his astrological knowledge with his herbal practice. In addition to plants, various parts of the body were believed to be under celestial influence. Because of this, a physician usually did not make a diagnosis or determine which plants to use before performing a series of complex astrological computations.

Just as today, there was scientific disagreement amongst herbalists in determining which celestial bodies influenced which plants. As a result, we sometimes have multiple associations. What does that mean for us if we incorporate astrological influences into plant magic? Like most things in a Pagan and Wiccan path, we need to work it out for ourselves if our magic is to be meaningful and powerful. Study the plants with which you want to work and their astrological influences, and then follow your intuition.

When astrological influences were originally determined, the planets consisted of five—Mercury, Venus, Mars, Jupiter, and Saturn—as well as the sun and moon, which were often referred to as luminaries. Of course since then the outer planets have been discovered, and modern astrology, quite naturally, includes them. Table 3 provides a brief overview of the aspects and attributes associated with the planets. Despite all the uproar in recent years, I have kept Pluto as a planet.

| Table 3. Planetary Aspects and Attributes for Magical Work | |
|---|---|
| Sun | Growth, manifestation, motivation, power, prosperity, protection |
| Moon | Creativity, emotions, fertility, guidance, love, transformation, wisdom |
| Mercury | Communication, inspiration, intelligence, messages, money, travel |
| Venus | Fidelity, friendship, love, passions, relationships |
| Mars | Action, courage, defense, lust, protection, sexuality, willpower |
| Jupiter | Authority, control, justice, luck, opportunities, success |
| Saturn | Ambition, discipline, goals, knowledge, loyalty, purification, strength |

| Table 3. Planetary Aspects and Attributes for Magical Work (continued) | |
| --- | --- |
| Uranus | Changes, community, goals, independence, inventiveness, motivation |
| Neptune | Adaptability, awareness, creativity, otherworld/underworld, vision |
| Pluto | The afterlife, karma, memory, renewal, sexuality, wealth |

## The Influence of Fixed Stars

While we know that twinkling is a way to tell the difference between a star and a planet, people in ancient times and up through the Middle Ages did not. They did, however, notice a difference in behavior and made an intelligent distinction. In medieval Europe, the stars and planets were called fixed stars and wandering stars, respectively. Fixed stars rose and set as did the moon, but they seemed to stay in the same pattern in relation to other stars. The planets were called wandering stars because their positions changed. They also seemed to move independently, unlike the stars of the constellations.

Medieval astrologers in Europe and the Middle East considered the fifteen stars noted by Agrippa as particularly powerful for magic. Heinrich Cornelius Agrippa (1486–1535) was the author of the most widely known manuscript on magic and the occult, *Three Books of Occult Philosophy*. Agrippa correlated the energy of certain plants commonly used in ritual and magic with the energy of stars in order to draw down their power.

Throughout the Middle Ages and the Renaissance, the use of fixed stars for magic and astrology was common practice, but because some stars have rather fatal or negative associations, the use of fixed stars in astrology gradually fell out of favor. However, modern astrologers have rediscovered these stars as a source of knowledge and have been using them as a way to add information to readings. Today, astrologers point out that the negative aspects ascribed to some stars simply serve as warnings and point to aspects of life that one may need to be particularly mindful.

| Table 4. The Fixed Stars | | |
|---|---|---|
| **Star Name** | **Constellation** | **Attributes** |
| Ala Corvi* | Corvus | Drive away evil spirits and all forms of negativity |
| Aldebaran | Taurus | Courage, honesty, intelligence, steadfastness, success |
| Algol | Perseus | The forces of the natural world, intense passion, strength |
| Alphecca | Corona Borealis | Quiet achievement, artistic skills, a change in social status that is earned, love |
| Antares | Scorpius | Defense, mindfulness of the potential for self-destruction, protection |
| Arcturus | Boötes | Exploration, leadership, protection, success in the arts, teaching |
| Capella | Auriga | Ambitions; public position; a warning not to let ambition, position, or wealth get out of hand; wealth |
| Deneb Algedi | Capricornus | The importance of balance, integrity, justice, wisdom |
| The Pleiades | Taurus | Communication with spirits, peaceful energy, inner knowledge, love |
| Polaris | Ursa Minor | Guidance, goals, protection against spells |
| Procyon | Canis Minor | Fame; mindfulness that fame, power, and wealth can slip away; power; wealth |
| Regulus | Leo | Authority, leadership, wisely used power, strength, success |
| Sirius | Canis Major | Communication, faithfulness, guardianship, passion, marital peace |

*The name *Ala Corvi* could refer to the stars Algorab or Gienah as both
of these names have shown up in various translations of Agrippa's work.

| Table 4. The Fixed Stars (continued) | | |
|---|---|---|
| Star Name | Constellation | Attributes |
| Spica | Virgo | Abundance, insight, knowledge, protection, psychic abilities |
| Vega | Lyra | Artistic talents, hopefulness, idealism, social awareness |

## Lunar Gardening

As our nearest celestial neighbor, the moon has influenced people more intimately than the planets and stars. We can see this in the fact that we celebrate it with our esbats. Gardening by the cycles of the moon helps us work with natural rhythms for planting, maintaining gardens, and harvesting. Lunar gardening is not as mysterious as it may sound. The moon's gravitational pull is well known for its effect on the tides. However, it also affects the underground water table and the flow of moisture in the soil.

There are four basic moon phases for lunar gardening. The first is the new moon, which is also called the dark moon. The other three phases in order of occurrence are waxing, full, and waning. To better understand what is going on during the phases, let's take a look at the positioning of the sun, earth, and moon, as well as the ocean's tides.

### The New Moon

The new moon brings a high tide to the ocean called a spring or moon tide. The word spring in this regard does not refer to a season. This word harkens back to its Old English usage, which meant to "grow" or "swell."[3] Likewise on land, the pull of the new moon draws underground water upward, bringing more moisture to the surface. This is considered a fertile time that is good to sow seeds, plant aboveground crops (such as tomatoes and Brussels sprouts), transplant garden plants or repot houseplants, and graft trees.

---

3  Sam Hinton, *Seashore Life of Southern California, New and Revised Edition* (Berkeley, CA: University of California Press, 1987), 19.

During this phase, the moon is between the sun and earth. (Refer to Figure 1.) The moon is pulling the sea and groundwater higher because it has the extra gravitational pull of the sun. The new moon is a quiet time, a time for divination and personal workings. This is a time for incubation and holding power.

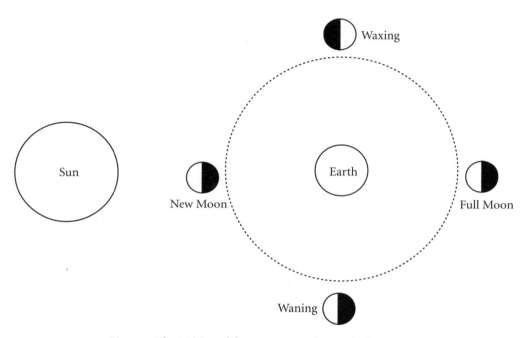

*Figure 1. The position of the moon varies during the four phases.*

### The Waxing Moon

Although the light of the moon is increasing during this phase, there is less gravitational pull than during a new moon. On the ocean, it causes a neap tide, which occurs on the quarter moons. From the earth, a quarter moon actually looks like a half moon. This is when the sun, earth, and moon form a right angle. The name for this tide also comes from Old English and means "scarce."[4]

---

4   Sam Hinton, *Seashore Life of Southern California, New and Revised Edition* (Berkeley, CA: University of California Press, 1987), 19.

Like the new moon, a waxing moon is considered a fertile time that is good to sow seeds, plant above ground crops, transplant garden plants or repot houseplants, and graft trees. It is a time of strong plant growth.

Magically, this is a time for growth, gathering knowledge, and inspiration. Much magic begun now culminates at the full moon. The waxing phase is conducive for creativity because of the high energy and clarity of vision it brings. It is also conducive for teaching.

### The Full Moon

The gravitational pull of the moon is actually downward during this phase. While the ocean is having another spring tide, the groundwater and water in the soil are being pulled down away from the sun. The sun, earth, and moon are in alignment again, but the moon is on the opposite side of the earth from the sun. However, they are not in perfect alignment, otherwise we would have a lunar eclipse every month. In this position, the moon is working against the sun's stronger gravitational pull.

For plants, the moon is pulling more moisture into their roots. This is the ideal time for planting belowground crops such as onions or potatoes. It is also a good time to pull weeds, thin out plants, prune, harvest, and mow.

Magically, the energy of the full moon is intense. This is a time for sending forth your will because of the high-powered energy that can propel it to manifest. This energy and bright moonlight occurs for three nights: on the night of the full moon, the night before, and the night after.

### The Waning Moon

Like the waxing phase, there is a neap tide and less gravitational pull during the waning moon. There is also a decreasing amount of moonlight leading into a rest period. Like the full moon phase, this is a good time to pull weeds, thin out plants, prune, harvest, and mow.

The waning phase is a time for turning inward and reflecting. It is a time for reaping what was put forth during the waxing phase. The waning phase is a good time for banishing spells and releasing what is unwanted. The decreasing moonlight carries away what we cast off.

## Parts of Plants and Their Symbolism

Through the centuries, herbalists discovered that different parts of plants served different purposes. In ritual and magic work, we often use various parts of plants because of their symbolism. For example, flowers are often used for love and sex magic, seeds for fertility, and fruit for abundance and manifestation. In addition to using a certain type of plant, you may find that coordinating a particular plant part with your purpose can add power to your spells and rituals.

Residing under the earth, roots are the most natural plant part for grounding energy and providing stability to our rituals and magic work. Roots also keep us grounded during psychic or astral work. As a symbol of longevity, roots encourage us to hold secrets when bidden. Roots offer access to the underworld, making them useful for connecting with ancestors, spirits, or chthonic deities.

Sturdy wood and bark from trees and the woody parts of other plants provide extra protective energy to rituals, spells, and charms. Wood and bark are also a gauge of growth and can aid us in manifesting our growth on various levels: social, emotional, and spiritual. Being at the center of or encircling a plant, wood and bark symbolically provide balance and bolster strength.

From the time they burst forth in the spring until the wind whisks them away in the autumn, leaves enfold the world with aerial enchantment. Personifying energy and growth, leaves give our magic and personal endeavors an encouraging boost. Showy or subtle, flowers are the crowning glory of plants. They represent beauty with a goal: attraction, sex, and fertility. Using flowers can be especially potent when they add fragrance to our magic work. It's no wonder that for thousands of years poets and lovers have sung the praises of flowers. Of course, leaves are often aromatic, too.

With the base word "fruit," fruition means completion or culmination, and so a piece of fruit symbolizes manifestation and success. Fruit represents an increase in power or energy. The feel and smell of fruit is the personification of abundance and freedom from want. Use fruit to increase what you have and to gain what you seek.

Seeds and nuts represent the beginnings of things and can be instrumental when encouraging something new in our lives. They also represent duality, such as the alternation between life and death, light and dark. Carried on a breeze or snuggled into the earth, seeds and nuts move between the worlds, representing beginnings, changes, and cycles.

## Our Relationship with Plants

We have a very fundamental, symbiotic relationship with the plant kingdom: plants provide us with oxygen and we provide them with carbon dioxide. In addition, plants have been vitally important for everything: providing food and medicine, materials for building shelters, and fibers for clothing.

In most ancient cultures, people believed plants to be magical, and for thousands of years they were used as much for ritual as they were for medicine and food. The presence of herbs in burial tombs attests to their power beyond medicinal purposes. Although the common concept of alchemy being the transmutation of base metal into gold, it was originally focused on plants and the search for the elixir of life.

Greek philosopher Aristotle (384–322 BCE) noted that plants had psyches. Also, there is an ancient Hindu belief that plants exist simultaneously in this world and the world of devas and other nature spirits. These ideas did not remain an ancient notion. In the 1970s, the Findhorn Foundation community in Scotland let it be known that it was through plants that they were able to contact and work with nature spirits. Working with plants for magic provides us with energy from the plants and access to nature spirits on whose aid we can call.

Spend a few minutes simply looking at a plant, and then place your hands on either side of it to sense its energy. If the plant is too large to do this, hold your palms facing it. If you are not sure what energy feels like, do this simple exercise first. Bring your hands together and rub your palms back and forth over each other until you feel them getting warm. This activates the chakras (energy centers) in your palms. Continue for another moment and then separate your hands to about shoulder-width apart. Slowly bring your hands closer together until you can feel a little bit of resistance.

Rub your hands together again, and when you separate them, move them toward each other and then away several times. As you do this, you may get the sensation that there is a ball between your palms that keeps them from touching. That's the feeling of energy. It is usually very subtle and it may take time to learn how to sense it. Working with houseplants is a good way to get started, and it will create good energy in your home.

When we tune into a plant's energy, we also share some of ours, which allows us to communicate with the plant and nature spirits. Taking time to be with and feel a plant's energy will let us know whether or not we may cut a piece from it. Respect is the most important aspect we bring to our relationship with the green world. If you get the feeling that you should not cut a piece from a plant, don't. Instead, gather parts that have fallen to the ground and leave an offering.

Over time as we work with plants, we may find that we are given additional information on how to employ them in our magic. When gathering plant material for a specific purpose, take time to visualize what you want to achieve as you connect with the energy of the plant. You may often receive details on what to do with each plant part. While this type of experience may be surprising, it is always gratifying.

And now, no matter which month you start in, begin your journey through the year with the magic of plants.

# January

After the lively revels of Yule, January is a quiet month. It opens the way to the new year and provides us with a fresh start. Whether or not we have made any resolutions, January presents the year as a clean slate upon which we can write our magic. This month was named for Janus, the Roman god of transitions and patron of portals.

## On the Calendar

### January 1: New Year's Day

The amaryllis is usually planted in late November or early December so it blooms in time for the holidays. However, planting one on New Year's Day is symbolic of starting the new year with a promise for the future.

..................

## Amaryllis

(*Hippeastrum* spp.)

    *Also known as: knight's star

The amaryllis is popular for its trumpet-shaped flowers that grow six to ten inches on stalks one to two feet tall. There are over seventy species of amaryllis and hundreds of hybrids and cultivars. Although these plants are not a true amaryllis, this name has been used for them for so long that there's no turning back.

The genus name *Hippeastrum* is Latin, meaning "horse star."[5] This is in reference to the large, unopened flower that resembles a horse's head especially when two of the plant's flat leaves stick up behind it like ears. The amaryllis has also been called knight's star because the shape of the fully opened flower resembles the brooch of certain orders of knighthood.

Once you have planted the amaryllis bulb, place it on your altar and say:

*As this year begins anew, and my dedication I renew. May the months ahead bring abundance and health; and everyone enjoy much peace and wealth.*

Leave the amaryllis on your altar for three days and then move it to a warm, sunny location. Although the flowers will not bloom in time for Imbolc, the phallic flower stalks make a good symbol of fertility for that sabbat's altar.

Amaryllis is associated with the element earth.

### January 6: Twelfth Night or Epiphany

Twelfth Night was originally a Pagan festival until the fourth century CE, when, like many Pagan celebrations, it was usurped into the Christian calendar. Traditionally, this day marked the end of the winter solstice revels. Also known as Epiphany, and usually associated with Christianity, the word actually has Pagan origins. Drawn from the Greek word *epiphaneia*, meaning "appearance," or "manifestation," in the Greco-Roman world

---

5    Robert Hogg, ed., *The Journal of Horticulture, Cottage Gardener, and Home Farmer, Volume VI: Third Series January to July 1883* (London: The Journal of Horticulture, 1883), 262.

it signified a deity visiting devotees in a sacred place as well as revealing him or herself in order to aid humans.[6]

Wassailing was traditionally done on this day to mark the end of the solstice revels. The term comes from the Old English *wæs hæl*, meaning "be healthy" or "be whole."[7] It was first used as a greeting, then a toast, and then for holiday door-to-door singing. Folklore has exploded with stories of singing, dancing, and a lot of drinking associated with wassailing. With as many wassail recipes as there are descriptions of old practices, what's a twenty-first century Pagan to do? Keep it simple and heartfelt, and take it back to the early custom of wishing a Happy New Year to the dryads who may inhabit your trees.

Cut or tear a couple of slices of bread into pieces and soak them in cider or apple juice. The amount of bread will depend on how many trees you have. When the bread is ready, go outside and place pieces on several branches or on the ground at the roots as you wish the tree and its spirit good health by saying:

*Wassail, dear tree and dryad. May this year ahead bring you much good health and cheer.*

..........................................................

## Masterwort and Angelica

Masterwort (*Imperatoria ostruthium* syn. *Peucedanum ostruthium*)

Angelica (*Angelica archangelica*)

Masterwort's genus name *Imperatoria* is Latin and means "ruler" or "master," and the plant was so named because of its healing properties.[8] The word master was once used as a title for physicians. In the Middle Ages, masterwort was cultivated in Europe and the root was widely used as a medicinal herb. Nowadays it is used mainly to flavor some drinks and as an ornamental plant. Associated with strength, courage, and protection, it was a

---

6 A. G. Martimort, I. H. Dalmais, and P. Jounel, eds., *The Liturgy and Time: The Church at Prayer: An Introduction to the Liturgy, Volume IV* (Collegeville, MN: Liturgical Press, 1986), 80.

7 Niall Edworthy, *The Curious World of Christmas: Celebrating All That Is Weird, Wonderful and Festive* (New York: Perigee Books, 2007), 23.

8 Christopher Cumo, ed., *Encyclopedia of Cultivated Plants: From Acacia to Zinnia* (Santa Barbara, CA: ABC-CLIO, 2013), 638.

custom in the Tirol region of Austria to ritually purify the house on this day by burning dried masterwort root.

Because masterwort is difficult to find and can be hazardous to handle, angelica makes a good substitute. In fact, masterwort is one of the common names occasionally applied to angelica. Angelica is also a good substitute because it comes from the same botanical family, *Apiaceae*, and even resembles masterwort. Both plants have strong protective qualities and are excellent for purifying and clearing negative energy. Refer to the entry in "December" for more information about angelica.

To purify your home, you will need a few small pieces of dried root. Place them in an incense burner or other heat-resistant container. As the root burns, walk through your house and waft a little bit of smoke everywhere. This will also freshen the rooms.

If you made a wish at Yule, write it down and burn it with some angelica root to seal your desire. Also, since this is the day of Epiphany, burn a little angelica to honor your chosen deity.

Angelica is associated with the element fire and the goddess Venus. Its astrological influence comes from the sun. Masterwort is associated with fire, and its astrological influence is Mars.

............
## HOLLY

American Holly (*Ilex opaca*)

English Holly (*I. aquifolium*)

   *Also known as common holly

On this day in parts of northwest England, it was customary to carry a flaming branch of holly through the town accompanied by a loud band and fireworks. On a much smaller and quieter scale, and since holly is associated with divinity, a few leaves can be burned to honor your special deity on this day of Epiphany. Write the name of a goddess or god on a holly leaf. Use additional leaves or a sprig of holly to honor multiple deities.

Go to a place outdoors where it is safe to burn things. Light a candle and then hold the leaves between your palms as you say:

*On this day of epiphany, I take time to honor thee. Your love and guidance I request; and through your power I will be blessed.*

Touch the holly to the candle flame and then drop it into your cauldron or other vessel. Repeat the incantation as the holly burns. When the ashes cool, scatter them on the ground.

Holly is associated with the elements air, earth, and fire. Its astrological influence comes from Mars and Saturn. It is associated with the following deities: Ares, Cailleach Bheur, Cernunnos, the Dagda, Danu, Freyr, Gaia, Holle, Lugh, and Saturn. For more information about holly, refer to the entry in "July."

### January 21: The Celtic Month of Rowan Begins

Rowan is the common name for these trees in the United Kingdom. In North America they are known as mountain ash. Although their leaves resemble those of the ash, true ash trees are in the genus *Fraxinus*.

..............
### ROWAN

American mountain ash (*Sorbus americana*)
   *Also known as dogberry, mountain sumac, and wild ash

Common mountain ash (*S. aucuparia*)
   *Also known as European mountain ash, quickbeam, sorb apple,
   witch wood, and witchen

Native to North America, the American mountain ash is a small, shrubby tree reaching fifteen to twenty-five feet tall. It has serrated, lance-shaped leaflets. They are dark green with gray-green undersides and turn yellow in the fall. The common mountain ash grows twenty to forty feet tall. It has medium-green, serrated, lance-shaped leaflets that turn yellow to reddish-purple in the fall. Both trees produce dense, flattened clusters of white flowers that bloom in May. After the flowers, orange-red berries develop and ripen in late summer.

In England during the fifteenth and sixteenth centuries, rowan had a negative reputation because it was linked with witchcraft. The most likely reason for this is because the berry carries a pentagram design at its base. Herbalists avoided using it for fear of being labeled a witch. Because rowan was associated with the storm god Thor, rowan was planted near homes and stables in northern Europe to protect the structures from lightning. In addition, rowan was used by the Celts when reciting magical incantations.

Write the name rowan or draw its ogham character on a candle for protection during rituals or astral travel. Rowan is a powerful ally for divination and for contacting elementals. Burn a small piece of bark or twig to enhance psychic abilities. Cut five branches to the same length and lay them out in a pentagram shape on your altar to attract success. Hold a rowan branch to connect with your spirit guides when seeking their advice. Rowan makes a good magically protective walking stick. Enhance its power by carving its ogham into the wood.

Rowan is associated with the elements earth and fire. Its astrological influence comes from the moon, Saturn, the sun, and Uranus. Rowan is associated with the following deities: Aphrodite, Brigantia, Brigid, Cerridwen, the Dagda, Hecate, Luna, Pan, Selene, Thor, and Vulcan.

*Figure 2. Rowan is associated with the ogham Luis.*

## In the Garden
### Witch Hazel
Witch Hazel (*Hamamelis* × *intermedia*)
   \*Also known as spotted alder, and winterbloom

There are several types of witch hazel; some bloom in the autumn, but the ones that flower in winter are the most dramatic. This particular species ranges from a large shrub to a small tree. It is a hybrid of the Chinese (*H. mollis*) and Japanese (*H. japonica*) witch hazels. The quintessential color of witch hazel flowers is yellow; however, some of these hybrids are orange or red. Resembling crinkled ribbons, these spidery flowers on bare branches brighten a dull landscape and are stunning in the snow.

Witch hazel's genus name comes from the Greek *hama*, meaning "together," and *mela*, "fruit."[9] Witch hazel seeds take a year to mature, which is why they appear at the same time as flowers. The "witch" in its common name comes from an Old English word that meant "to bend," in reference to its pliant branches.[10]

---

9   Glyn Church, *Trees and Shrubs for Fragrance* (Buffalo, NY: Firefly Books U.S. Inc., 2002), 74.

10  Ernest Small and Paul M. Catling, *Canadian Medicinal Crops* (Ottawa, Canada: National Research Council of Canada, 1999), 64.

Collect a few witch hazel flowers and tuck them into a sachet for love divination, or place them in your work area when you seek inspiration. Let the flowers dry and then burn them for protection spells or banishing rituals. Place a couple of small witch hazel twigs on your altar or table during divination sessions to help focus your mind and open psychic channels. Hold a branch to aid in communicating with deities. Hanging a branch over the front door provides protection to your home. Burn dried flowers, bark, or a twig to aid in recovering from loss. After a relationship breakup, waft smoke of the bark in each room of the house to remove the presence of the person who left. Burn a few flowers for a healing circle or ritual to strengthen the energy you send out.

Witch hazel is associated with the elements earth, fire, and water. Its astrological influence comes from Saturn and the sun.

*Figure 3. Witch hazel is associated with the ogham Emancoll.*

## In the Wild
### *Eucalyptus*
Blue Gum Eucalyptus (*Eucalyptus globulus*)
    *Also known as fever tree, gum tree, southern blue gum,
    and Tasmanian blue gum

Although eucalyptus is often planted as an ornamental tree, it has made itself at home in the wild. This tree can grow over three hundred feet tall in its native habitat of Australia and Tasmania, but in California and other places where it was introduced it reaches half that size. It is called gum tree in reference to the sticky gum-like substance that the tree secretes. The smooth, brown bark peels in large pieces leaving patches of bluish-white and giving the tree a mottled look. Its blue-green, lance or oval-shaped leaves become long, narrow, and yellowish on mature trees. From November to April, feathery, yellowish-white flowers grow at the leaf axils. The flowers give way to top-shaped seedpods that take about eleven months to mature. The small seeds can be black, brown, orange, or tan.

In the nineteenth century, eucalyptus was introduced from Australia into California, southern Europe, Egypt, South Africa, and India.[11] Its oil is a powerful antiseptic and familiar to most people for treating colds.

Eucalyptus is best known for its powers of purification. Burn dried leaves to dispel negative energy and consecrate your ritual space. Wear a sprig of leaves or flowers as an amulet for protection against emotional upsets during past-life work. Use eucalyptus oil in the home to raise the spiritual vibration. (Refer to the entry in "February" for instructions on how to make a reed diffuser.) Dried leaves and flowers facilitate dream and psychic work and communication with spirits. The scent of eucalyptus increases concentration for spell work.

Eucalyptus is associated with the elements air, earth, and water. Its astrological influence comes from Mercury, the moon, Saturn, and the sun.

## In the House
### House Plant Magic
While there is not a lot for many of us to do in the garden or find in the wild in January, houseplants can become the focus for plant magic.

..............................

### AFRICAN VIOLET
(*Saintpaulia ionantha*)

African violets come in a wide variety of sizes, shapes, and colors. This species is the quintessential plant with rounded, dark green leaves that grow from a center crown. Stalks with clusters of purple flowers also grow from the center. African violets are a good choice for winter blooming; in fact, given the right conditions, they bloom well all year.

Closely associated with the home, African violets lighten the energy and invite blessings. Position one wherever you want to lift and move energy. One or two in a front window will draw abundance into your home. Place one with dark blue or purple flowers on your altar to raise the spiritual vibration of meditation or ritual. Use dried purple flowers in love charms and white flowers to attract love.

---

11    Andrew Chevallier, *The Encyclopedia of Medicinal Plants: A Practical Reference Guide to Over 550 Key Herbs and Their Medicinal Uses* (New York: Dorling Kindersley Publishing, 1996), 94.

African violet is associated with the element water. Its astrological influence comes from Venus.

..........
## ALOE
(*Aloe vera*)
 *Also known as medicine plant

Aloe is a perennial plant with succulent leaves that can grow up to two feet long from a center base. If you are lucky, it will produce a spike of yellow or orange flowers. Aloe is commonly kept in kitchens for first aid. The clear gel from a broken leaf is especially good for burns. A yellow sap known as bitter aloe is exuded at the base of the leaves. Bitter aloe should not be used on the skin.

In the Middle East and Egypt, aloe was regarded as a holy symbol with which to protect the home. As such, leaves were hung over doorways. In addition to protecting the home, aloe was believed to provide protection from accidents and bring good luck.

If you live in an area where it can grow outdoors, plant aloe near your front door to ward off negativity and attract good luck. Otherwise, grow it on a windowsill at a front window for the same purpose. For home protection, break open the end of a leaf and dab a little of the clear gel over each exterior doorway. When performing spells for healing, dab a little of the gel at the base of a green candle. For your esbat ritual, dab the gel on a white candle or put the whole plant on your altar to draw down the wisdom of Luna.

Aloe is associated with the element water. Its astrological influence comes from Jupiter, the moon, and Venus.

................
## BAMBOO
(*Dracaena sanderiana*)
 *Also known as lucky bamboo and ribbon dracaena

Although this woody evergreen looks like and is called bamboo, it is not a true bamboo. However, known as lucky bamboo, it carries a number of its namesake's attributes. This plant has a slender upright stem and graceful, arching leaves that taper to a point. It can be grown in a vase of water with pebbles to keep it upright or planted in soil.

Place the plant in a room where your family gathers to engender peace and congeniality. Position it near the main entrance to your home to invite luck and harmony. Also for luck, hold the vase or pot of bamboo between your hands and make a wish. Position the plant beside or near your altar to draw its energy into your rituals and meditations. It can also be used to disperse negative energy or spells that have been sent your way.

Bamboo is associated with the element air and the god Thoth. Its astrological influence comes from the sun.

. . . . . . . . . . . . . .

## Cactus

Barrel Cactus (*Echinocactus grusonii*)
  *Also known as golden ball and golden barrel cactus

Bunny Ears Cactus (*Opuntia microdasys*)
  *Also known as polka-dot cactus

Although there are hundreds of different kinds of cacti, the bunny ears and barrel are two of the most popular. Bunny ears are easy to recognize because of their flat, paddle-shaped stem segments from which new segments form. These new segments tend to form in pairs that give this cactus a rabbit-like silhouette. It is dotted with clumps of spines that grow in a polka-dot pattern on the pads. The barrel cactus was so named for its barrel or globe shape. It has a golden crown of woolly hairs and prominent spines along protruding ribs that run from top to bottom on the plant.

If you live in an area where you can grow cacti outdoors, it is usually recommended to place one at each corner of the property. Alternatively, one planted just outside each exterior door can accomplish the same intent for protection. Similarly, when grown as houseplants, position one near each exterior door or in a window on each side of the house.

The sharp, needle-like spines of a cactus can be used in protection spells. Using tweezers, carefully remove a few from different areas of the plant. The spines can be buried at the corners of your house or wrapped in a small sachet that can be hung inside. Also, the sachet can be taken along when you travel for protection no matter where you go.

Cactus is associated with the element water. Its astrological influence comes from Mars.

## CYCLAMEN

*(Cyclamen persicum)*
  \*Also known as florist's cyclamen and sow bread

With long, graceful stems, cyclamen flowers seem to float above the rest of the plant. The flowers range from white to many shades of pinks and reds. The leaves are rounded with marbling. In regions where it can be grown outdoors, it usually blooms in late winter or early spring. The folk name sow bread comes from the practice of feeding the roots of this plant to pigs.

Associated with fertility and lust, the root has been dried, powdered, and baked into little cakes as an aphrodisiac as well as to make someone fall in love. It has also been used to attract love.

Incorporate the plant into the decor for a handfasting ceremony, or sprinkle petals on the wedding bed. To keep the fires of passion burning, use the plant as a centerpiece or strew a few petals on the table for anniversary dinners. Cyclamen is also associated with protection and sleep. In addition to sparking love, a plant in the bedroom can protect the sleeper from negativity and banish nightmares.

Cyclamen is associated with the element water and the goddess Hecate. Its astrological influence comes from Venus.

## FERN

Boston Fern *(Nephrolepis exaltata)*
  \*Also known as sword fern

Maidenhair Fern *(Adiantum raddianum)*
  \*Also known as rock fern

Cousin to the woodsy male fern *(Dryopteris filix-mas)*, the Boston fern is the most common indoor fern. In Victorian times, this plant was a hallmark of graceful parlors and porches. Boston ferns are long-lived plants that can reach several feet tall and wide.

Among the most-loved ferns, the maidenhair offers fine-textured fronds on black stalks. The arching fronds emerge light green and darken slightly as they age. This plant's association with hair comes from the folk belief that drinking tea made from this fern would keep one's hair from falling out.

In general, ferns have been associated with sensuality and fertility, and were believed to bestow perpetual youth. Because of their ethereal fronds and shaded habitats, ferns have been associated with fairy magic and enchantment.

Place a fern on your altar to aid in connecting with the fairy and other realms. Closely aligned with the elements air and earth, ferns can lighten and lift energy while keeping you grounded. Save dried fronds when you prune them from the plant. These can be burned to clear negative energy and banish unwanted spirits. Also use them in protection spells against hexes.

Fern is associated with the elements air and earth. Its astrological influence comes from Mercury.

······················

## GERANIUM

Common Geranium (*Pelargonium* × *hortorum* syn. *P. inquinans*)
   *Also known as bedding geranium and zonal geranium

Loving the sunshine, geraniums can be found on countless windowsills and porches. Their flowers and foliage come in a range of colors. The leaves often have distinct bands or zones of color, which is the source of the name zonal geranium. The flowers can have single or double blooms in pink, white, red, or salmon. The genus name comes from the Greek *pelargos,* meaning "stork," which refers to the plant's elongated seed casings that resemble a stork's bill.[12]

Geraniums are vigorous plants that stir energy and foster growth. Tuck a leaf into your pocket to enhance psychic energy, or position a potted plant nearby when traveling in the astral realm. For protection, place a couple of red geraniums on a windowsill in the direction from which you feel a threat. Also associated with focus and success, position one of these plants on or near your desk or wherever you work on anything creative or financial in nature. Burn dried leaves or flowers to aid in breaking hexes.

Geranium is associated with the element water, and its astrological influence comes from Venus.

---

12   Barbara J. Euser, ed., *Bay Area Gardening: 64 Practical Essays by Master Gardeners* (Palo Alto, CA: Solas House, 2005), 105.

....................

## GOOSEFOOT

(*Syngonium podophyllum*)

*Also known as arrowhead vine

The goosefoot is an evergreen climbing vine that grows three to six feet long. A young plant has upright stems but as it ages it develops climbing stems. The common names for this plant come from the shape of its leaves, which are dark-green with silvery white or cream variegation. The leaves go through a dramatic change in shape as the plant matures. They begin with the goosefoot or arrowhead shape and then develop three or five narrow sections. Goosefoot produces greenish-white flowers, though rarely as a houseplant.

With arrow-shaped leaves, this plant is an aid for defensive magic. Position it in your home wherever you feel the need for protection. Crumble and burn a dried leaf for spells or energy work when seeking transformation. Hold or use a fresh leaf in ritual to connect with the goose-footed goddess Freya.

Goosefoot is associated with the element air and the goddess Freya. Its astrological influence comes from Jupiter.

....................

## SPIDER PLANT

(*Chlorophytum comosum*)

This plant gets its name from its spider-like appearance and its spiderettes or "babies" that dangle from the mother plant like little spiders on a web. The spiderettes start out as small, white flowers. Once it develops roots, the spiderette can be planted to start a whole new colony of spider plants. Spider plants have solid green or variegated leaves, and they are good for clearing impurities from indoor air.

Representing the element air, these plants absorb negativity while improving and lifting the energy of your home. Hang one wherever you feel energy has gotten bogged down. A plant with many babies symbolizes fertility and abundance. Hang it in the bedroom if you are planning on a pregnancy, or root one of the babies in its own pot and place it next to your bed. Hang a spider plant in a kitchen window to invite prosperity into your home.

## Winter Wellness with Thyme

A steaming cup of herbal tea is just right for warming up on a cold January night. Thyme is also perfect for adding a flavor of summer to meals and for fighting colds.

..............

### THYME
(*Thymus vulgaris*)
    *Also known as common thyme, English thyme, and sweet thyme

Growing up to fifteen inches tall, thyme is a perennial shrub with a base stem that becomes woody with age. It has gray-green oval leaves and small pink to lilac or bluish-purple flowers that grow in little clusters. Thyme grows well in the garden and on a windowsill, making it handy for wintertime use.

Thyme is one of the classic herbs in Mediterranean cuisine that dates back to ancient times. The Greeks and Romans not only used this herb in cooking but also as a healing antiseptic. Thyme was an ingredient in a range of remedies, and it was used to fumigate homes to avert infectious diseases.

Today this herb is used for a range of respiratory problems, including chest colds, wet coughs, hay fever, sinusitis, sore throat, and tonsillitis. The warming and drying properties of thyme are an aid for clearing congestion. Use the tea as a mouthwash and gargle, which will fight throat infection, gingivitis, and bad breath. Not only does this herb fight infection, it also provides support for the immune system and eases digestive complaints.

### Thyme to Warm Up Tea
1–2 teaspoons dried thyme

1 cup boiling water

Steep the tea for ten minutes and strain. For variation, use one teaspoon of thyme and one teaspoon of sage or rosemary.

Although thyme is a common herb, it is a powerhouse for magical purposes. It is well known for its purification properties, which make it ideal for preparing ritual space and consecrating altars. Sprinkle dried leaves on your altar to stimulate energy for divination and psychic work, including any type of work involving the fairy realm. Wear a fresh sprig when making contact with the otherworld. Also use thyme to clear negative energy in general and to enhance awareness for clairvoyance. Use dried leaves in a sachet to increase the effectiveness of spells involving love, luck, and money. Stuff a little dream pillow with thyme leaves and/or flowers to help remember and interpret your dreams.

Thyme is associated with the elements air and water. Its astrological influence comes from the planet Venus and the fixed star Capella.

# February

While the night of the year draws to a close, February can sometimes bring the most severe weather of the season. However, the promise of spring becomes palatable when receding snow begins to reveal greening grass. Seeds that have been resting in Gaia's womb slowly make their way to the surface to sprout in the sunlight. This month was named after the ancient Roman ritual of purification, *februum*, which was held mid month.[13]

## On the Calendar
### *February 2: Imbolc/Midwinter*
At Imbolc we are halfway between winter solstice and spring equinox. It is a time when the days become noticeably longer. This sabbat is a celebration of the reawakening of the earth. It is also a time of purification and clearing out unneeded things from

---

13    Paul J. J. Payack, *A Million Words and Counting: How Global English is Rewriting the World* (New York: Citadel Press Books, 2008), 175.

our lives. As the world is beginning to awaken from winter's slumber, it is time to shed the past and move forward with hope and growth.

If you planted an amaryllis bulb on New Year's Day, place it on your Imbolc altar to symbolically stir the energy of life. Later in the month when the amaryllis has bloomed, place it on your altar again to use in love spells or sex magic. A red amaryllis is especially effective for this purpose.

Brigid's cross is a fundamental symbol of this sabbat. It is an ancient type of design called a whirl, which symbolically stimulates the energy of life to begin a new cycle. Straw that is set aside from autumn mulching works well to make the cross. Most of the straw that we get at garden centers comes from cereal grains such as barley and wheat, which are grains associated with Demeter. The use of straw at Imbolc is a symbol of hope and promise for the future as it foreshadows the story of Demeter and Persephone at Ostara.

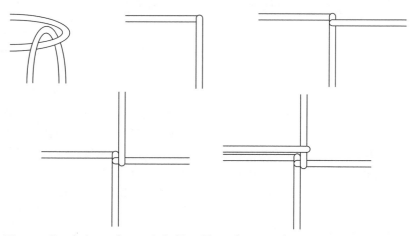

*Figure 4. Bend pieces of straw in half and loop them together to create Brigid's cross.*

Soak the straw in water overnight so it will be pliable and can be bent without breaking. To make a Brigid's cross, bend two pieces of straw in half, loop them together, and then position them at a ninety-degree angle to each other. Take another piece of straw and bend it in half around the vertical piece so the three pieces form a slightly off-centered letter "T." Do the same with a fourth piece, bending it in half around the third piece at a ninety-degree angle. These pieces form the center of the cross. Continue adding one or two pieces of straw to each side of the cross.

To finish, set the cross down on a flat surface and place something heavy enough to hold the center in place. Trim the end of each arm to the same length, and then tie a piece of yarn or string around the ends to hold each arm together. After the straw dries, add a longer piece of yarn to hang the cross, or simply place it on your altar.

### February 14: Valentine's Day

This is a day for expressing love as well as for love spells and charms. The Victorians turned the language of flowers into a fine art, and nothing says love like the rose. Although the Victorians are regarded today as prudish, the rose was a popular buttonhole flower that sent a signal about male sexual prowess. In ancient times, this flower was considered the perfection of nature in symmetry and harmony. It was a symbol of Aphrodite, Venus, Isis, Ishtar, and Astarte. According to Greek legend, a drop of Aphrodite's blood gave the rose its red color. In addition, roses were said to have been a component in Cleopatra's arsenal of seduction.

For centuries, drying and preserving roses was done to perfume the home in winter. At this time of year, most of us will have to turn to florist shops for fresh roses. Instead of putting them all in a vase, take a few flowers apart and sprinkle the petals on the dinner table and/or on your bed to celebrate Valentine's Day. When searching for that special someone, turn around in a circle as you sprinkle rose petals and say:

*Rose petal, rose petal, fragrance so sweet; with your power my love I will meet.*

Rose essential oil can also be used in place of dried or fresh flowers. Use roses in any form to attract love, heighten desire and passion, and to increase fertility and fidelity. For more about roses, refer to the entry in "July."

### February 18: The Celtic Month of Ash Begins

In Norse mythology, the World Tree Yggdrasil was an ash that connected heaven and earth. Ash is associated with the Celtic god Manannan, and according to myth, this tree came from his undersea realm. Along with oak and hawthorn, ash was considered part of the triad of powerful fairy trees. In addition, it was reputedly the favored broom handle wood for witches' besoms.

........
## Ash

Common Ash (*Fraxinus excelsior*)

*Also known as European ash and Venus of the woods

White Ash (*F. americana*)

*Also known as Biltmore ash and cane ash

The common ash reaches eighty to one hundred thirty feet tall, and the white ash fifty to one hundred feet tall. They have straight gray trunks and dense crowns of foliage. The name ash comes from the color of the bark. Each leaf stem sports nine to thirteen leaflets that are lance shaped and slightly serrated. Small greenish-yellow flowers produce clusters of seeds that remain on the tree until spring when they are blown off. Also called keys, the flat seeds are oval and straight, unlike the maple seed, which is curved.

Collect a few ash keys for your altar and make a circle around the base of a candle upon which you have carved ash's associated runes and/or ogham. Use this setup during divination sessions or to boost the energy of spells. Wrap a few keys in a soft cloth and place it under your pillow at night to aid in dream work. Ash provides connection with other realms, whether dreaming or journeying.

Light a candle inscribed with the ogham or any of the runes, and place it on your desk or workspace when seeking creative inspiration. Use the keys in protective spells and charms against any form of negative magic. Burn a small ash twig for love spells.

Ash is associated with all four elements, and its astrological influence comes from Mercury, Neptune, the sun, and Uranus. This tree is associated with the following deities: Ares, Belenus, the Dagda, Freyr, Frigg, Holle, Macha, Mars, Minerva, Neptune, Odin, Poseidon, and Thor. It is also associated with fairies and elves.

*Figure 5. Ash is associated with the ogham Nion and the runes Ansuz, Ehwaz, Gebo, Hagalaz, and Wunjo (shown left to right).*

## In the Garden
### Black Hellebore
(*Helleborus niger*)
> *Also known as Christmas rose

Black hellebore is a bushy, clump-forming perennial. Its glossy, dark green leaves are deeply lobed and lance shaped. The white flowers are cup shaped with overlapping petals. While it may seem odd that a plant with white flowers has the word black in its name, it was so called because of the color of its roots.

This plant's genus name was derived from the Greek *helein*, meaning "to take away," and *bora*, "food."[14] This describes its use in the ancient world to induce vomiting. Black hellebore is very toxic if taken internally, and it is a skin irritant. Even bruised leaves can cause severe dermatitis. Needless to say, wear gloves if you handle it, and more importantly, don't grow it in your garden if you have children.

With all that said, why grow it? This plant has a long history with witchcraft and sorcery. The Greeks and Romans used it to bless cattle and to keep them free from spells. In the Middle Ages, the roots were considered magical and strewn on floors to banish evil spirits. In addition to warding-off witches, it was believed to be used by witches for placing hexes and for enabling them to fly. In France it was believed that sorcerers would grind the roots into a powder and scatter it in the air to render them invisible.

In addition to historical links, another reason to grow black hellebore is that this plant seems to defy winter. Although not traditionally associated with Cailleach, draw a circle on the ground around your black hellebore as you say three times:

*Cailleach, great crone of winter, mother of darkness whose stories are told, bless this plant, keep safe my garden; protect us through the storms and cold.*

Black hellebore is associated with the element water. Its astrological influence comes from the planet Saturn and the fixed star Algol.

---

14    Katherine Kear, *Flower Wisdom: The Definitive Guidebook to the Myth, Folklore, and Healing Powers of Flowers* (London: Thorsons, 2000), 98.

### Crocus

Early Crocus (*Crocus tommasinianus*)

    \*Also known as Tommies and woodland crocus

Snow Crocus (*C. chrysanthus*)

    \*Also known as golden crocus

Dutch Crocus (*C. vernus*)

    \*Also known as giant crocus and spring crocus

Known for its colorful, chalice-shaped flowers, crocus is a signal that spring has made a foothold. Long thin leaves that resemble blades of grass grow from the base of the plant. They are dark green with a central white or silvery stripe. The early crocus flowers are pale lavender to reddish-purple with a white throat. The snow crocus flowers are yellow-orange and sometimes have maroon markings. Dutch crocus can be purple or white.

The name of this plant is derived from the Greek *krokos*, meaning "saffron."[15] The spice saffron comes from the autumn-blooming crocus (*C. sativus*). According to one ancient legend, this flower was named for a beautiful youth named Crocus who was consumed by his love for a shepherdess. Another story explains that these flowers first blossomed on a hillside after Zeus and Hera made love there. According to later folklore, the devil was said to be mortally afraid of crocus.

Crocus flowers do not last long when cut, so it is usually easier to use dried ones. Place dried flowers in a small sachet to use in a charm to attract love, or place the sachet under your pillow at night to banish nightmares. Crumble dried flowers and leaves into a powder to sprinkle at the corners of your house to bless your home and promote peace within. Also, sprinkle a tiny pinch of the powder on an incense charcoal before a divination session to enhance clairvoyance. As it burns, say three times:

*Spring flower, gentle crocus; share your power, help me focus.*

Crocus is associated with the element fire and the goddess Eos. Its astrological influence comes from Venus.

---

15    Allen J Coombes, *Dictionary of Plant Names* (Portland, OR: Timber Press, Inc., 1985), 64.

## Cypress
Italian Cypress (*Cupressus sempervirens*)
>   *Also known as common cypress, graveyard cypress,
>   and Mediterranean cypress

Originating in southern Europe and western Asia, the Italian cypress is widely used for landscaping in North America. This evergreen conifer grows in narrow, columnar form forty to sixty feet tall. It has dark gray-green, scale-like foliage on upright branches. The foliage is aromatic when crushed. Round, knobby cones grow in clusters. Native to North America, the Monterey cypress (*C. macrocarpa*) is an endangered species. The bald cypress (*Taxodium distichum*) and others in its genus are deciduous trees, not evergreens.

The cypress was highly valued for medicinal and religious purposes in ancient times. The genus *Cupressus* is the Latin name for this tree. Although there are a number of versions of the Greek myth concerning a young man named Cyparissus, the gist of them all is that he was heartbroken after accidentally killing a beloved, tame stag. His grief was so great that he was transformed into a cypress tree, which at that time was already a symbol of sorrow. Despite its association with death and mourning, two cypress trees planted on a property were said to bring peace and prosperity to a household.

Cypress is a powerful ally when dealing with death and loss, especially to provide comfort and healing. Use a sprig on your altar to remember and honor ancestors and other loved ones. Burning a piece of cypress wood is effective for centering and grounding energy before and after a ritual. Also burn it for defensive magic, or to consecrate and bless ritual objects. Cypress is supportive of spells that banish, bind, or provide protection. Hold a branch in ritual or meditation when seeking truth and knowledge, or to stimulate growth and renewal. Holding a couple of cypress cones fosters awareness and clarity for divination and channeling. Place a branch of cypress on your altar for strength and wisdom when seeking justice. Hang one over your front door for protection.

Cypress is associated with the elements earth and water. Its astrological influence comes from Pluto and Saturn. This tree is associated with the following deities: Aphrodite, Apollo, Artemis, Astarte, Cupid, Diana, Hades, Hecate, Jupiter, Pluto, and Saturn.

## *Snowdrop*

Common Snowdrop (*Galanthus nivalis*)
  *Also known as Candlemas bells, fair maid of February,
  snow princess, and white queen

One of the earliest flowers to peek out at the barren landscape, the snowdrop's drooping, white blooms often come up through a blanket of snow. The snowdrop has narrow, grass-like leaves surrounding the flower stems. The pendulous flowers are white with three inner and three outer petals. The inner petals have a touch of green at their tips. The genus name *Galanthus* is derived from the Greek *gala*, "milk," and *anthos*, "flower."[16] The species name *nivalis* is Latin for "snowy."[17] Like many popular garden plants, the snowdrop has many species and hybrids.

In England and Scotland, the snowdrop was considered a flower of hope because it was a sign that spring was on its way. The number of inner and outer petals, a doubling of the sacred number three, also makes it a symbol of hope. Despite this association, bringing one flower into the house was considered bad luck in some parts of England, but taking in more than one was not.

To the Victorians, the snowdrop was a death token because the flowers were so close to the ground—belonging more to the dead than the living. However, folklore is fickle because it was also believed that if snowdrops grew under the windows of a house, the family within would have happiness.

Make a wish when you see the first snowdrop of the season, but do not pick it. Place an offering amongst snowdrops to make contact with the nature spirits and devas. Burn dried leaves in spells and rituals to build strength when you are faced with difficult issues. Also do this when you need help to persevere in a situation. Dried flowers in a sachet can be carried with you to bolster bravery and dispel fear.

Snowdrop is associated with the element earth.

---

16  Kear, *Flower Wisdom*, 56.

17  *Ibid.*, 57.

## In the Wild

### *Coltsfoot*

(*Tussilago farfara*)
   *Also known as coughwort

Growing along stream banks, dirt roads, and wasteland areas, coltsfoot sends up yellow, dandelion-like flowers from February to June. Like dandelions, coltsfoot flowers turn into fluffy, white seed balls. The name coltsfoot comes from the rounded, hoof-like shape of its leaves. Because the leaves open after the flowers go to seed, it is sometimes difficult to identify this plant.

Both the Greeks and Romans used coltsfoot medicinally. The Romans treated coughs with it and named it *tussilage*, meaning "cough dispeller."[18] In place of a trade or professional sign, an image of the coltsfoot flower was painted on doorposts of apothecary shops during the Middle Ages.

Coltsfoot is associated with Brigid and can be used to honor her at Imbolc. To honor Epona, pick four leaves and press them in a book. When the leaves are dry and flat, place them on your altar to represent hoof prints. Place three flowers or leaves in a sachet bag to wear as an amulet, which will help to increase psychic abilities and enhance your visionary experiences. Also, the amulet can be placed under your pillow to aid in dream work. Crumble dried flowers and leaves together and then sprinkle them where you need to dispel negative energy. Sprinkled outside your front door, coltsfoot will invite a peaceful and calm atmosphere into your home.

Coltsfoot is associated with the element water and the goddesses Brigid and Epona. Its astrological influence comes from Venus.

### *Wolfberry*

Fremont's Wolfberry (*Lycium fremontii*)
   *Also known as desert thorn and thornbush

This member of the nightshade family (*Solanaceae*) blooms in the Desert Southwest and southern California. The thicket-forming wolfberry grows about five feet tall

---

18   Dobelis, *Magic and Medicine of Plants*, 146.

and six feet wide. Its succulent leaves are spatulate shaped and share branches with thorns. The tubular, five-petaled flowers range from lavender to purple. In the summer, the flowers give way to reddish-orange fruit, which look like cherry tomatoes.

Place a handful of flowers on your altar to invite new friendships and loyalty into your life. Make a sachet of dried flowers to place under your pillow for dream work and to help manifest your dreams. Tie a small piece of black ribbon in each of the cardinal directions on the branches of a wolfberry bush as you ask for its protection. Also, the thorns can be used for protection and defensive magic.

Wolfberry is associated with the element water.

## In the House
### Essential Oils for Magic

February is a good time to work with essential oils. Not only do they add fragrance to the air, they also connect us with the natural world and provide another way to engage in plant magic. While the use of essential oils may seem more New Age than Pagan to some people, these oils come from plants, and down through the ages witches and Pagans have used plants and oils for magic and ritual. As their name implies, essential oils carry the essence and life force energy of a plant.

When I create magical blends of essential oils, I like to set the intent from the very beginning. After I assemble all my blending gear, I draw a pentagram with a felt-tip pen on a paper towel on my work surface. While I'm doing this, I like to chant or say an incantation such as:

*Green world, green world, abundant and pure; bring forth your strength, beauty, and more. Green world, green world, please assist me; manifest my will, so mote it be.*

While these words are general in nature, you can include something specific about the purpose of a blend you create. Essential oils are popular for consecrating candles and tools, and you might want to create special blends for certain sabbat or esbat rituals. If you use essential oils on objects, the ones that you hold for any length of time during ritual will release fragrances as your body heat activates the scent.

As an alternative to putting oils directly on magic or divination tools, put a few drops of your blend on a small cotton ball and place it where you store these items. This will allow them to slowly absorb the vibrational energy of the oil without causing damage, which essential oils can sometimes do. Also, in the lead-up to actually doing a spell, use a cotton ball with your special oil blend and store it with the things you will use for the spell. This will give them time to steep in the scent as well as your intention.

If bathing before ritual or magic work is part of your practice, adding essential oil to the water is a good way to amplify the bath's purification purpose. Use twelve to thirteen drops of your essential oil blend in an ounce of carrier oil, and then add it to your bath. See the section below for creating magical bath oils and salts.

Scenting an area before and during ritual, magic, or psychic work is another way to harness the vibrational energy of the plants from which the essential oils came. This is easily done with a diffuser. While electronic diffusers, nebulizers, and all sorts of gadgets are available in a range of sizes and prices, the low-tech tea light candle lamp does the job nicely. Besides, candles enhance the ambiance of ritual and craftwork.

Taking a cue from the ancient Egyptian use of incense, I like to use oil blends as an altar offering. Sometimes I do this as part of ritual and other times to simply honor a deity. Place a few drops of oil in a small bowl and chant or recite an incantation to announce its purpose. An offering of this type can precede magic, divination, or psychic work to vibrationally smooth the way.

Oils are often used to consecrate gemstones and crystals, too. The synergistic energy will boost the vibrational energy of the stone and the oil. A tiny dab is all that is needed. Avoid bathing the stone in oil as this may subdue some of its features, such as any optical phenomenon.

Special oil mixes can be used as house blessings or for other important occasions. Protective blends can be dabbed over doorways or anywhere you feel the need for it. You can also make a blend for any type of energy boost. And, of course, forget about the air fresheners on the market. Make your own, which will keep your house scented as well as magical. See the section below for making a reed diffuser.

## MAGICAL BATH OILS AND SALTS

Cold winter nights are conducive for long soaks in the tub, and essential oils enhance the experience. In the bath, essential oils help to relieve stress, pain, and muscle ache. A carrier oil provides even distribution of the essential oil when it is to be used in water. For a healing beauty bath, mix essential oils with milk instead of using carrier oil. The fat in milk acts like a carrier oil and absorbs essential oils, which become diluted as they are dispersed throughout the milk. Use twelve to thirteen drops of essential oil in an ounce of carrier oil or milk, and then add it to your bath water.

In addition to carrier oils and milk, essential oils can be mixed with salts. Epsom salts are healing and make a good medium for essential oils. Coarse sea salt can also be used. Salts contain minerals that aid in the release of toxins from the muscles and joints and promote relaxation.

### Basic Recipe for Bath Salts

2 cups Epsom or sea salts

2 tablespoons baking soda (optional)

10–15 drops essential oil

Place the dry ingredients in a glass bowl. Plastic should be avoided as chemicals from the plastic container can leach into the oils. Add the essential oil and mix thoroughly. Store the bath salts in a glass jar with a tight lid. The optional baking soda in the ingredient list helps to soothe the skin. To use the salts, add a handful or two under the running tap to dissolve them.

For a Valentine's Day blend, try a combination of lavender, chamomile, rose, lemon, anise, and cedar. If you are making bath oil, try almond or apricot for the carrier oil. For a bath of renewal at Imbolc, combine rosemary, thyme, pine, and lemon with almond or olive oil as the carrier. When making your oil blend or bath salts, charge them with a chant or special incantation to suit their intended purpose.

## FRESHEN THE AIR WITH A LITTLE MAGIC

For many of us, opening the windows to air out the house is not feasible at this time of year. Although there are a plethora of "air fresheners" on the market, many of us prefer not to use chemical-based, artificial scents. A gentle way to scent the air is to use a reed diffuser. It takes a little longer than an electronic diffuser or tea light lamp to disperse the essential oil into the air, but it is a nice, subtle method to freshen and renew the energy of a house.

**Things needed to make a reed diffuser:**

A glass or porcelain container

Reeds

Carrier oil

Essential oil(s)

A short glass or porcelain jar or vase with a narrow neck works best. A wide-mouthed jar with a cork can be adjusted by drilling a hole in the cork so it is large enough to accommodate the reeds. There are several types of reeds on the market, however, rattan reeds work best as they are porous and wick the oils more evenly. The reeds should be at least twice the height of the jar.

Choose lightweight carrier oil for the base, as thicker ones are not drawn up the reeds as easily. Sweet almond oil is often recommended, but I have found that sunflower, a very thin oil, works best. If you are using more than one essential oil, blend those together first and then give them about a week for the scent to mature.

Pour a quarter cup of carrier oil into your diffuser jar, add two teaspoons of the essential oil or oil blend, and swirl to mix. Place the reeds in the jar and turn them a couple of times the first day to diffuse the scent. After that, turn them once a day or every other day. Over time, you will need to add more oil to the jar, and when the reeds become saturated, replace them.

There are several things to avoid when making a reed diffuser. First, the fragrance oils on the market for reed diffusers are synthetic and not essential oils. Some of them may smell nice, but they are made from chemicals, not plants. The commercial base oils for reed diffusers are also usually chemical-based. Mineral oil and dipropylene glycol are sometimes recommended as a base, but avoid these for the same reason.

Wait a couple of days until the reeds are drawing up the oils, and then carry your diffuser around your house as you say:

> *Winter soon will be done, as spring draws forth the warming sun. Clear this home of all things stale; blessed renewal, welcome and hail!*

# March

Signs that the earth is awakening become visible as the bonds of winter are loosened. This windy month blows away the staleness of winter, and with it we cast away the things we need to remove from our lives. This season brings freshness and new perspective as the increasing sunlight brings warmth and renewed life. March was the first month on the ancient Roman calendar, and it was named for Mars, the god of war.

## On the Calendar

### March 17: Saint Patrick's Day

While this day celebrates a Catholic saint, there is a lot of Pagan symbolism that we can celebrate. One symbol is the shamrock, or clover. The Celtic triskele design might have been based on the clover. Although the triskele was adopted by Christians to illustrate their trinity, it was long believed that three-part things or something repeated three times was magical and carried special energy. In addition, the shamrock is associated with the spring equinox and represents triple goddesses. In medieval times it was a symbol of true love.

### WHITE CLOVER

(*Trifolium repens*)

*Also known as Dutch clover, moon clover, and trefoil

Blooming from March through December, the tiny white to pale pink flowers are clustered into somewhat spherical flower heads that suggest a lunar influence. Clover leaves consist of three leaflets. Occasionally, four-leafed clovers can be found, which was believed to enable the finder to see fairies and to break enchantments. English botanist Maxwell Masters (1833–1907) made an interesting notation about four-leafed clover. "*Trifolium repens* was gathered at night-time during the full moon by sorceresses … while young girls in search of a token of perfect happiness made quest of the plant by day." [19]

Gather three stems of leaves to place on your altar for help in grounding and centering after ritual or psychic work. Pick one stem of leaves, wrap it in a tissue, and press it in a book until it is dry. Keep this in your wallet to attract and increase abundance in your life. Clover flowers and leaves are an aid in banishing fear and protecting from hexes.

Leaving the stems long, pick enough flowers so you can tie them end-to-end to make a crown. Wear this when beginning a spell to attract love, and then place it over your bedpost for three nights. On the fourth night, burn the crown as you send your energy out to the universe.

Clover is associated with the elements air and earth. Its astrological influence comes from the planet Mercury, and the fixed stars Alphecca and Spica.

*Figure 6. Clover is associated with the rune Othila.*

### *March 18: The Celtic Month of Alder Begins*

Although the alder has served a wide range of domestic uses, it has also been regarded as highly magical. It is also a healing tree for its forest companions in the wake of disasters.

---

19   Maxwell T. Masters, *Vegetable Teratology: An Account of the Principal Deviations from the Usual Construction of Plants* (London: Robert Hardwicke, 1869), 356.

............

## Alder

Common Alder (*Alnus glutinosa*)
    *Also known as black alder and European alder

Alder grows about sixty-five feet tall and often has multiple trunks. Slender, drooping male catkins (clusters of tiny flowers) and small, pinecone-like female catkins appear before the leaves develop. The female catkin produces a small nut. The glossy green leaves are rounded, heavily veined, and notched at the end.

Young, green branches are easily turned into whistles by cutting both ends and pushing out the pith with a smaller stick. These hollow branches can be cut to various lengths and tied together to create panpipes, which were named for the Greek god Pan. Whistles made from this wood are said to be magical and have the ability to summon the four winds.

If you have an alder on your property, leave an offering for fairies beneath it as they are said to be attracted to this tree. Collect a handful of catkins for magic work. Burn them for aid in banishing rituals and spells, or crumble them onto your altar for water, wind, and general weather magic. A leaf under your pillow will invite prophetic dreams. Hold three leaves between your palms before a divination session to bring clarity. Holding a branch of alder helps to connect with spirit guides. Use a small twig as a protective charm by keeping it in a small decorative bag that you can carry with you or keep in your car.

Alder is associated with the elements air, fire, and water. Its astrological influence comes from Mars and Venus. This tree is associated with the following deities: Cailleach Bheur, Freya, Manannan, Minerva, and Venus.

*Figure 7. Alder is associated with the ogham Fearn (left) and the rune Isa (right).*

### March 20/21: Ostara/Spring Equinox

This sabbat celebrates both the sun and the earth. It marks the balance of all things, female and male, the spiritual and the physical. It is a celebration of rebirth, as life seems to burst forth everywhere and the earth turns lush and green. Any type of flower is appropriate for the ritual altar; however, branches of Forsythia are especially apropos. Its four-petaled, cross-shaped flowers represent the elements, the balance of the equinox, and the union of male and female. The bright yellow color is symbolic of the sun and the increasing warmth of the season.

......................

### Forsythia

(*Forsythia × intermedia*)

   *Also known as border forsythia and golden bells

Forsythia is a rambling shrub that can reach eight feet tall and ten feet wide. Long, arching branches are a hallmark of this plant. The yellow flowers grow in clusters making the branches look like golden sprays. When the flowers fade, oval-shaped leaves with serrated edges fill in the branches, creating a rounded thicket.

Forsythia flowers seem to burst onto the scene to remind us what this sabbat is about. Use the flowers in charms to increase fertility, or if already pregnant, place them on your altar as an offering and thanks. Put several cut branches in a vase of water and place it in your home where you need to activate and lift energy.

Forsythia is associated with the element air.

## In the Garden

### Bluebell

Virginia Bluebell (*Mertensia virginica*)

   *Also known as jacinth and Virginia cowslip

Bluebell is a common name given to different plants. In America we have the Virginia bluebell, in England bluebell refers to the wild hyacinth (*Hyacinthoides non-scripta*), and in Scotland bluebell is another name for harebell (*Campanula rotundifolia*).

The large, oval leaves of the Virginia bluebell are light to grayish green and somewhat floppy. Growing on nodding stems, the flowers start off pink and gradually turn a vivid shade of light blue as they mature. Whether naturalized in a garden or found in the wild, the ephemeral beauty of these flowers creates a magical sea of color. It is no surprise that these enchanting little bell-shaped flowers are associated with fairies.

According to legend, treading on bluebells would result in being pixie-led, which means that a person would be led away by fairies or pixies. He or she would not be able to escape the fairies until another human came to the rescue. Bluebells were also said to aid in seeing fairies.

Growing bluebells in your garden is a way to attract fairies to your property and draw luck into your life. These flowers also aid in manifesting what you desire. Write what you seek on a piece of blue paper, and then burn it in your cauldron. When the ashes cool, scatter them among the bluebells as you visualize your desire. The same method can be used for overcoming an obstacle. Wearing bluebell flowers is said to prompt a person to speak from the heart. This can be instrumental for lovers to determine if they are right for each other, but this should be used carefully as truth carelessly spoken can seem hurtful.

Bluebell is associated with fairies.

### Daffodil
(*Narcissus pseudonarcissus*)
   *Also known as daffadowndilly, jonquil, and narcissus

Although there is a popular story that this flower was named for the Greek youth who fell in love with his own reflection, the name *Narcissus* comes from the Greek word *narkao*, meaning "to be numb."[20] It is also the basis for the English word narcotic.

According to Greek legend, daffodils were said to have carpeted the Elysian Fields, a blessed otherworld. In other legends, these trumpet-shaped flowers heralded Persephone's return to this world and the beginning of spring. There was also a belief that daffodils found in the wild indicated the location of an ancient sacred site.

Daffodils growing in a garden bring protection to the home and clear away negative energy. For specific help, cut a daffodil, dip the flower head in a bowl of water, and then sprinkle it around the outside of your home as you say three times:

*Daffodil, daffodil, hear my call; against negativity, build a wall.*

---

20   Richard Alan Miller and Iona Miller, *The Magical and Ritual Use of Perfumes* (Rochester, VT: Destiny Books, 1990), 97.

State what you need protection from or the negativity that needs to be removed, and then repeat the incantation three more times. Carry the bowl with you so you can continue sprinkling water as you recite the incantation. This method can also be used to remove spells.

Although the daffodil is associated with death, it carries the energy of rebirth and renewal, and it is a good flower to include on your Ostara altar. A bouquet of daffodils in the house brings luck, love, and blessings to the home. However, the bouquet should consist of at least three flowers to avoid bad luck. The daffodil is also a symbol of friendship.

Daffodil is associated with the element water and the goddess Persephone. Its astrological influence comes from the sun and Venus.

### Dogwood
(*Cornus florida*)
  *Also known as flowering dogwood

This small tree is an attention-getter when it comes into bloom. However, what appears to be large, white, notched petals are actually bracts (modified leaves) that protect the tiny, greenish-white cluster of flowers in the center. Because dogwood blooms at this time of year, it is commonly used on Ostara altars. Cut a couple of boughs to drape over your altar or scatter some of the large white bracts across the altar top.

This tree's genus name comes from the Latin *cornu*, meaning "horn" because of the hardness of its wood.[21] Its common name, dogwood, has nothing to do with canines; in fact, early on the tree was called dagwood. In Germany, the wood was used to make skewers and other pointed tools as well as sturdy animal prods called "dags" (with the "a" sound as in "father").[22] In America, the name dagwood evolved into dogwood.

Dogwood is associated with making wishes come true and has been used in charms for getting one's own way. The energy of this tree is known to engender loyalty and fidelity. Carry a small piece of twig to foster this in the people around you, but only if

---

21  Barbara G. Hallowell, *Mountain Year: A Southern Appalachian Nature Notebook* (Winston-Salem, NC: John F. Blair, Publisher, 1998), 89.

22  *Ibid.*

you are deserving of it. Sitting under a dogwood is said to inspire new ideas and to help view a situation in a new light. To call on the protective aspect of this tree, place a few of its white bracts under your welcome mat to serve as guardians of your home. Because we now call it *dog*-wood, think of them as acting as guard dogs.

Dogwood's astrological influence comes from Mars.

### Pansy
Garden Pansy (*Viola* × *wittrockiana*)

Wild Pansy (*V. tricolor*)

    *Also known as heartease and Johnny-jump-ups

Garden pansies are viola hybrids developed from the wild pansy. There are now more than two hundred cultivars of pansies. These flowers can be single or multi-colored and with or without markings. The most common types of pansies have a dark center called a "face." The wild pansy is smaller than its garden cousins, and often has thin black lines called "whiskers" radiating from the center of its face. Both of these pansies are cousins to violets.

The wild pansy was named heartease from its long use in love charms. Carrying one of its flowers was said to ensure that your sweetheart returned your love. The name pansy comes from the French *pensée*, which means "thought."[23] In the Victorian language of flowers, pansies were given with the intention of being remembered or thought of. With this same intention, give a potted bowl of garden pansies to your lover or someone whose attention you would like to attract. If that is too bold for the situation or not possible, pick a pansy flower and tape or clip it to a picture of him or her as you say:

*Pansy dear, pansy sweet; may this one be my love to meet.*

Because pansies are most fragrant at early morning and dusk, use them during these times of day to boost spells. Dawn and dusk are in-between times that support magical energy and give access to other realms. Place wild pansy flowers on your altar when engaging in love divination. Sprinkle flower petals in your bath water to aid in attracting

---

23    Sheila Pickles, *The Language of Flowers* (London: Pavilion Books Limited, 1990), 75.

love. Also, hold a few flowers or a potted plant in your hands to deepen meditation or reflection, especially when seeking your life's purpose.

Pansy is associated with the element water. Its astrological influence comes from Saturn.

*Figure 8. The Wild Pansy is associated with the rune Gebo.*

### Violet

Common Blue Violet (*Viola sororia* syn. *V. papilionacea*)
   *Also known as meadow violet and wood violet

Sweet Violet (*V. odorata*)
   *Also known as English violet, garden violet, and sweet pansy

Cousins to pansies, violets form clumps that can be four inches tall and six inches wide. Their leaves and flowers grow on separate stems directly from the rhizome. The flowers consist of five rounded petals: two upper, two out to the sides, and one lower petal. Violet leaves are wide, oval to heart-shaped, and gently serrated. The flowers of the common blue violet are blue-violet or white with purple veining. The flowers of the sweet violet are dark purple but occasionally white.

According to Roman legend, Cupid adored violets, which were all white, but Venus was envious and turned them purple. These flowers were extremely popular in ancient Greece and were sold in Athenian street markets. Along with lilies and roses, Romans used violets to adorn tombs.

In medieval times, the delicate powdery aroma of violets was used to scent linens. Young girls in London street markets commonly sold bouquets of these flowers. Violets were believed to be an antidote to evil spells and witchcraft in general. However, it was considered bad luck to pick the flowers if they still had dew on them.

Violets are associated with sleep and support dream work. Wrap a couple of flowers in a tissue or soft cloth and place them under your pillow as you say three times:

*Violet flowers, scent so sweet; aid my dreams as I sleep.*

Because violets often bloom in the snow, they are a symbol of hope and can invite happiness into your life. Place a handful of flowers in a small vase on your altar when seeking change and to help your wishes come true. Also associated with fairies and elves, violets can aid in connecting with these magical beings. Use a stick to draw a circle around a clump of violets when they first begin to sprout to signal that your garden is a safe and welcoming place for fairies. Also leave an offering of milk.

Violet is associated with the elements air and water. Its astrological influence comes from Venus. This flower is associated with fairies and elves, and the following deities: Aphrodite, Attis, Venus, and Zeus.

## In the Wild
### Adder's Tongue
Northern Adder's Tongue (*Ophioglossum pusillum*)
   *Also known as adder's fern and serpent's tongue

American Trout-lily (*Erythronium americanum*)
   *Also known as adder's tongue and dogtooth violet

There is a lot of confusion over the name adder's tongue because the American trout-lily shares it as a folk name. As previously mentioned, this confusion has extended to the point where the folk name dogtooth violet has been applied to northern adder's tongue. As a result, these plants have been used interchangeably in magic.

Although it is in the same family as ferns, northern adder's tongue does not resemble its cousins and actually looks snake-like. It has one oval leaf-like frond and one seed stalk, which looks like a double row of beads that turn reddish as they mature. This plant grows between five and twelve inches tall, and can be found in marshes, ditches, and woods that are seasonally wet. Its genus name comes from the Greek *ophios*, meaning "serpent," and *glossa*, meaning "tongue."[24]

The American trout-lily grows in colonies where each plant has a pair of brownish, mottled leaves (spotted like a trout) at the base of a stalk that bears a solitary, yellowish

---

24   Margaret Grieve, *A Modern Herbal, Volumes 1 and 2* (Mineola, NY: Dover Publications, 1971), 309.

flower. The drooping flowers have dark protruding stamens. According to folklore, this plant was said to cure snakebites. The name dogtooth violet refers to the shape of its white underground bulb. This plant can be found in moist deciduous woodlands and clearings.

American trout-lily is associated with the moon. Use the flowers to support divination and lunar magic. Include a few flowers in a sachet and place it under your pillow to aid in dream magic. In the nineteenth century, it was considered an aphrodisiac.

Northern adder's tongue is an aid for emotional and spiritual healing, and for deepening spirituality. This plant also helps to bolster strength and courage. Gather and dry a couple of oval leaves to burn in spells for these purposes, or place two of the seed stalks on your altar and meditate on your purpose.

In some areas, these plants are considered endangered species. Check with your local or state government. If this is the case, they should not be collected, of course. Instead, if you find them, take a moment or two to sense their energy, and then state your purpose for seeking their aid. Send them healing, supportive energy before you leave.

Adder's tongue is associated with the element water. Its astrological influence comes from the moon.

### Bloodroot

(*Sanguinaria canadensis*)
    *Also known as Indian paint, red root, and tetterwort

The bloodroot rhizome sends up single leaves from which a flower emerges on its own stem when the leaf unfurls. The palm-shaped leaves have five to nine lobes and are yellowish-green with orange veins. They are pale green underneath. Up to two inches across, the flower has a yellow center and eight to sixteen white petals. The flowers appear from late February to early May. Bloodroot is found in moist woodlands and along woody slopes.

The genus name *Sanguinaria* was derived from the Latin *sanguis*, meaning "blood."[25] This is in reference to the reddish-brown or orange-colored sap from the rhizome. Both the rhizome and the sap are considered unsafe to ingest because of potential side effects.

---

25   Laura C. Martin, *Wildflower Folklore* (New York: The East Woods Press, 1984), 91.

Despite this, the rhizome was used medicinally by Native Americans to treat fever and other ailments, and it was listed as an official botanical drug in the United States until 1926. Although it is no longer considered safe for herbal medicine, bloodroot is considered an ornamental garden plant.

Place dried leaves and/or flowers in a sachet to use as a charm for protective love. Sprinkle crumbled, dried leaves in the woods to release attachments. Burn a dried leaf to bolster courage or to add strength to spells. Place a flower or leaf on your altar to aid in divination. For esbat and women's rituals, place three flowers on your altar.

This plant is endangered or threatened in some states. If this is the case where you live, work with its energy and leave an offering. Do not take any part of it.

Bloodroot is associated with the elements fire and water. Its astrological influence comes from Mars and the moon.

### Dandelion
(*Taraxacum officinale*)
   *Also known as devil's milk pail and wild endive

So much time, energy, and money has been spent on trying to rid the world of dandelions, yet they persist. Although it is now considered a weed, European settlers introduced it into North America as a food crop and medicinal herb. The name dandelion is a mispronunciation of the French name for it, *Dent de Lion*, "tooth of the lion."[26] It was so named because of the jagged shape of its leaves.

The use of young dandelion leaves in salads prompted the name wild endive. The name devil's milk pail refers to the sticky, white sap that oozes from the broken root. Being underground, roots were often considered property of the devil by Christians. Pagans and Wiccans associate the dandelion with Hecate. Although the long taproot is notoriously difficult to pull out, extract the root of a small plant. Let it dry out, and then burn it to honor Hecate, or use it as an amulet.

---

26   Susan Wittig Albert, *China Bayles' Book of Days: 365 Celebrations of the Mystery, Myth, and Magic of Herbs from the World of Pecan Springs* (New York: Penguin Group USA Inc., 2006), 110.

Appropriate for Ostara, the dandelion is a plant of balance with its yellow flower spreading out like a little sun, and then developing into a seed head that is white and round as the moon. Every child knows the summer fun and powerful magic of blowing on the dandelion seed head and making wishes. Individual seeds floating on the air were called "wishers" and were considered lucky if caught. Pick a seed head at night and make a wish in the moonlight with the power of Luna to aid you. Before blowing on it, say:

*Dandelion seed head, round and white; bring the wish I make this night.*

In addition to granting wishes, dandelion seed heads were used as a type of oracle to tell time. According to folklore, after blowing on it, the number of seeds left indicated the hour of the day. The same method was also used to find out how many children you would have. By whispering into the seed head and then blowing in the direction of one's lover, dandelions were said to carry amorous messages.

The dandelion is associated with the element air and the goddesses Brigid and Hecate. Its astrological influence comes from Jupiter and Mercury.

### Yucca
Mojave Yucca (*Yucca Schidigera*)
   *Also known as Spanish dagger

Adam's Needle (*Y. filamentosa*)
   *Also known as Spanish bayonet

These are two of the many species of yucca that grow in the wild in dry, desert areas. They are also used in landscaping, and small ones are kept as houseplants. Mojave yucca is an evergreen shrub with a few upright branches that become tree-like over time. Adam's Needle remains low to the ground. Both of these plants have sword-like leaves that measure two to four feet long and spires of cream-colored, bell-shaped flowers.

In South America, yucca plants are associated with earth goddesses. Collect a few flowers to place on your altar to honor Gaia. Yucca is also associated with increasing spiritual awareness, transformation, and protection. Scott Cunningham suggested braiding several yucca fibers into a hoop to wear as a crown for shape shifting.[27] Also do this for astral travel or working with the fairy realm. Make a larger hoop of fibers to hang on your front door as a wreath, and decorate it with other plants associated with protection. Instead of a wreath, dry and then hang two leaves like crossed swords as a protective talisman.

Yucca is a cleansing plant that aids in removing hexes, jinxes, or any negativity. Make an infusion by chopping a piece of root into small bits. Simmer it in water for twenty to thirty minutes. Let it cool and then strain. Sprinkle the liquid around your home and property, or on yourself as you visualize all things negative melting away.

Yucca is associated with the element earth and earth goddesses. Its astrological influence comes from Mars and Pluto.

## In the House
### Candied Violets
One way to extend your enjoyment of violets is to candy the edible flowers. This applies to the common blue violet (*Viola sororia*) and sweet violet (*V. odorata*). Be sure to collect the flowers from an area that was not sprayed with pesticides.

### A Recipe for Candied Violets
40 flowers

2 drops almond or vanilla extract

1 egg white, frothy

1 tablespoon water

½ cup confectioners' sugar

Gently rinse and drain the flowers. In a bowl, combine the extract, water, and egg white. Gently brush mixture onto violets to coat. Sprinkle with enough sugar to completely cover. Dry them in the oven at 200 degrees Fahrenheit for about twenty to thirty minutes. When cool, store them in a glass or porcelain container.

---

27   Scott Cunningham, *Cunningham's Encyclopedia of Magical Herbs* (St. Paul, MN: Llewellyn Publications, 1998), 228.

Use the flowers to top a dessert or enhance a salad. They can also be used for sweetening a love spell.

### Get Seeds Started

Get a jump on spring planting by sowing seeds indoors. Look for seed packets that have both the common and scientific names as well as planting instructions.

Items needed for starting your plants from seed include seed trays that are divided into sections, potting soil mix, and a spray bottle. Consider recycling plastic egg cartons for seed trays. Other alternatives to seed trays are peat or newspaper pots, which are biodegradable and can be planted directly in the ground outside where they will decompose. A potting soil mix is a blend of mediums that aids seed germination. A spray bottle is good to use because the seeds need to be kept moist, but you don't want to drown them.

Soak the seeds in water overnight, which will help them to germinate. Before placing them in the water, cup them in your hands as you say:

*Tiny seeds, I soon will sow; with love and magic may you grow.*

The next day, place a little potting mix in the seed tray, drop in several seeds per compartment or pot, cover with soil, and use the spray bottle to gently water them. As you do this, you may want to chant to imbue the seeds with your magical intention.

Most seed trays come with a lid, and if you are using the clear plastic egg crates, they have built-in lids. Otherwise, use a piece of plastic wrap and make a tent over your seed pots. Covering them helps to create a warm, moist atmosphere. Place them in a warm, dark spot, which will aid the germination process. Check them every day for sprouts.

When seedlings begin to appear, remove the lid or tent, and keep them in a warm, bright spot but out of direct sunlight. If there are multiple seedlings per compartment, remove some of them and leave only the strongest one or two. After the seedlings develop several sets of leaves, transplant them into separate small pots so the roots will have room to develop. Put soil in the pot and make a well in the middle. Remove a seedling from the tray with a teaspoon and carefully place it in the pot. Gently fill in soil around the roots. Continue to keep the plants moist but not wet.

If you are using the biodegradable peat or newspaper pots, you will not have to re-pot the seedlings. Let the plants develop for at least a few more weeks before moving them outdoors.

# April

As the weather warms and flowers blossom, it should be no surprise that the name of this month comes from the Latin word *aprilis*, which means "to open."[28] April is the month when life seems to burst forth as the earth turns many shades of lush green. Each rain shower seems to bring more plants to life, and flowers of every hue open to the sun. This rigorous life-force energy feeds our bodies and spirits and awaits our magical direction.

## On the Calendar
### April 15: The Celtic Month of Willow Begins
Usually found near water, willows are linked with sacred and mysterious powers, enchantment, and death. They are associated with in-between times, which is why they are used at both Beltane and Samhain.

---

28   Payack, *A Million Words and Counting*, 175.

················
## Willow

American Willow (*Salix discolor*)

   *Also known as pussy willow

Weeping Willow (*S. babylonica*)

Both of these trees have narrow, lance-shaped leaves that are finely toothed. The American willow is nicknamed pussy willow due to its fuzzy, gray catkins that resemble the soft pads of cat's feet. It is a shrubby, multi-stemmed tree that grows from six to fifteen feet tall with leaves that are dull, green above and lighter underneath. The weeping willow is widely loved for its long, graceful branches that sweep down to the ground. It can grow thirty to fifty feet tall with a crown that can be just as wide. Its catkins are silvery green, and its leaves are light green above, gray-green beneath.

Although a Christian tradition in England, Russia, and Eastern Europe, it would not surprise me if this custom had its roots in Pagan practice. Palm Sunday was often referred to as Pussy Willow Sunday because instead of importing palm fronds, local pussy willow branches were taken to church on the Sunday before Easter. In fact, in England the plant itself was sometimes called the English palm. After the branches were blessed, they were taken home and placed with religious icons or hung in the house. Branches from the previous year were then burned. As an early-blooming plant, pussy willows were believed to have "special productive and protective powers."[29] Place a vase of pussy willows on your altar or hang a silver-tufted branch in your home to call on this plant's powers of protection and fertility.

These water-loving trees are also associated with the moon. Make a circle with pussy willow catkins and/or willow leaves on your April esbat altar to aid in raising lunar energy. Willow is allied with all moon goddesses as well as Danu and the Morrigan.

To empower love spells and divination sessions, take a thin weeping willow branch, strip off the leaves, and wind it into a circle. Tie short pieces of yarn in several places to keep the circle intact, and then set it on your altar. Draw the willow ogham or rune on a pink or red candle for love spells, or draw them on a white candle for divination. Place the candle in the middle of the willow circle, and as you light the candle, say:

---

29   Linda J. Ivanits, *Russian Folk Belief* (New York: Routledge, 2015), 8.

*Willow, willow, tree of enchantment; graceful branch now circled and round. Bestow your power and your wisdom; in this endeavor, willow knowledge abound.*

Once you befriend this tree, it is very generous and will provide you with many wands and other gifts. Willow dryads tend to be curious, sometimes shy, but always welcoming. They can aid you in contacting fairies and other nature spirits.

Willow is associated with fire and water. Its astrological influence comes from the moon and Venus. This tree is also associated with fairies, and the following deities: Artemis, Athena, Belenus, Brigid, Ceres, Cerridwen, Danu, Diana, Hecate, Hera, Hermes, Ishtar, Loki, Luna, Mercury, the Morrigan, Osiris, Persephone, Poseidon, Rhiannon, and Zeus.

*Figure 9. Willow is associated with the ogham Saille (left) and the rune Laguz (right).*

### April 28: Floralia

The Roman celebration of Floralia was named for Flora, the goddess of spring and flowers. It was a festival of fertility that was usually expressed through sexual practices. Place flowers or sprinkle petals on your altar. This is a good day for working spells of love, lust, and fertility. Crabapple flowers, daisies, primrose, geraniums, and violets are especially effective.

### April 30: May Eve/Walpurgis Night

Like Floralia and Beltane, Walpurgis Night was a celebration of spring and fertility, and a night of lusty revelry. Like Samhain, May Eve is one of those special nights of the year when the veil between the worlds is especially thin. According to folklore of the British Isles, this is when the fairy folk come out of their mounds and return to our world. In addition, because the hawthorn provided good branches for broomsticks and witches were said to congregate under these trees, people were warned to stay away from hawthorns on this night. Decorate your altar with hawthorn or any type of flower.

*April 30: National Arbor Day*

This day focuses on revitalizing forestland and planting more trees in cities and towns. It is a good day to send out magical energy to support the green world. It is also a good time to visit your favorite tree or woods.

## In the Garden

*Cherry*

Black Cherry (*Prunus serotina*)
  *Also known as rum cherry

Sweet Cherry (*P. avium*)
  *Also known as bird cherry and wild cherry

Black cherry has glossy, oblong leaves with pointed tips and serrated edges. Its fragrant, white flowers hang in pendulous clusters. In late summer its fruit turns a deep, purplish-black. While bitter to eat right from the tree, these cherries make excellent jams and pies. The leaves and bark have a distinctive cherry-like odor when crushed. While the fruit of the sweet cherry is not exactly sweet, birds love them, which is why it is called the bird cherry. Its species name *avium* is Latin for "bird."[30] This tree has fragrant, white flowers and dark, oval leaves with serrated edges.

Cherry trees are a symbol of abundance. They also attract good luck. Place cherry blossoms on your altar when performing spells to stimulate and attract love. In a bridal bouquet the flowers foster a long, happy marriage and increase fertility. Burn a piece of bark as incense to heighten awareness during divination sessions. Press a cherry blossom in a book, and when it dries out, keep it in your wallet to help overcome an obstacle. When the obstacle or situation is resolved, burn the flower as you affirm your gratitude for this tree's help.

Cherry is associated with the elements fire and water. Its astrological influence comes from Mercury and Venus. This tree is also associated with the following deities: Artemis, Flora, Mars, the Morrigan, Pan, Persephone, and Thor.

---

30   Ernest Small, *Top 100 Food Plants: The World's Most Important Crops* (Ottawa, Canada: National Research Council of Canada, 1999), 149.

## Crabapple

American Crabapple (*Malus coronaria* syn. *Pyrus coronaria*)

   *Also known as sweet crabapple and wild crabapple

The crabapple is a small tree with a short, crooked trunk. This unassuming little tree puts on a great display of flowers that can range from white to pink to rose-tinged. The flowers grow in groups of two to six on short, spur-like branches. The leaves are oval and coarsely toothed. In August, the little green crabapples become noticeable, and in the autumn they turn red as they ripen. Less than two inches across, the fruit is edible but slightly bitter or sour. For these reasons, crabapples are usually overlooked for eating; however, when cooked they make excellent jams, jellies, fruit fillings, chutneys, and applesauce.

The Celts used their native crabapple for food and for the production of an alcoholic drink. This tree also held an important place in Celtic mythology. The legendary Avalon, Isle of Apples, and the place where King Arthur was taken to recover from his wounds, was most likely populated by wild crabapple trees. In weather folklore, a heavy crop of fruit in the autumn means a hard winter will follow.

Use crabapple blossoms in spells to invite abundance and prosperity to your home. Before performing a spell to attract a lover, prepare yourself with a bath by sprinkling a handful of flower petals in the water. When you are finished bathing, collect the petals and place them in a bowl on your altar.

When interacting with fairies, carry a branch or wand made from a crabapple tree as it helps open the way to their realm. The branch also provides magical protection. Additionally, hold a branch or wand while doing spells for protection or hang it over your altar. When seeking knowledge to make an important decision, light a candle and meditate as you sit in front of your altar holding a crabapple leaf in each hand.

Associated with Beltane, crabapple blossoms are a traditional and symbolic flower to place on the sabbat altar. If your tree blooms too early for the sabbat, place a few flowers in a container in the freezer, and then bring them out just before your ritual.

Crabapple is associated with the elements air and water. Its astrological influence comes from Venus. This tree is associated with fairies and the following deities: Aphrodite, Apollo, Athena, Badb, Cailleach Bheur, Diana, Dionysus, Eros, Flora, Freya, Hera, Lugh, Macha, Manannan, Rhiannon, Venus, and Zeus.

*Figure 10. Crabapple is associated with the ogham Quert (left) and the rune Inguz (right).*

### Daisy
Common Daisy (*Bellis perennis*)
  *Also known as bairnwort, day's eye, English daisy, and wild daisy
Ox-eye Daisy (*Leucanthemum vulgare* syn. *Chrysanthemum leucanthemum*)
  *Also known as marguerite

While daisies are garden favorites that come in every color of the rainbow, these two have the classic white petals. They are the daisies most often used in magic and can be found in the wild. The common daisy has a small flower with a yellow central disc from which white petals radiate. The flowers are only about an inch wide and grow on stems that are one to four inches tall. Its small, spoon-shaped leaves grow in flat rosettes. This flower can be found in lawns and meadows.

Also sporting a yellow, central disc and radiating white petals, the ox-eye daisy holds its flowers aloft on stems that are one to three feet tall. Long, lance-shaped leaves grow from the base of the plant while small, toothed leaves grow along the flower stems. The ox-eye was originally imported as an ornamental plant, but it is now naturalized in meadows, along roadways, and in marginal areas.

The common name daisy comes from their name day's eye, which was derived from the Anglo-Saxon *dæges eage*.[31] They were called day's eye because they open during the day and close at night. Used to bless babies in Scotland, daisies were called bairnwort.

---

31  Kear, *Flower Wisdom*, 7.

In Scotland, *bairn*, refers to a child.[32] In addition, it was believed that putting a daisy chain around a child's neck would prevent him or her from being carried off by fairies.

The Victorians considered the daisy a child's flower to pick, make chains with, and play games. The daisy was also regarded as a symbol of fidelity and was of value in the divination of one's love affairs by performing the familiar one-by-one plucking of petals.

The traditional way to make a daisy chain is to slit the lower part of a flower stem with your thumbnail, and then thread another stem through it. Make a small daisy chain and hang it over your child's bed as a protective amulet. Or, put it over your own bed if you want to attract love.

Because daisies are associated with the goddess Freya, weave a daisy chain and place it on your altar to honor her. The ox-eye daisy is associated with Artemis and the moon. Place a few of these flowers under your pillow to enhance dreams and to aid in interpreting messages received during sleep. Dreaming of daisies in the spring is said to bring good luck. Grow daisies in your garden to invite the blessing of fairies and to communicate with them.

Daisy is associated with the element water. Its astrological influence comes from the sun and Venus. The ox-eye daisy is influenced by the moon. Daisies are associated with fairies and the following deities: Aphrodite, Freya, Thor, Venus, and Zeus. The ox-eye daisy is also associated with Artemis.

### Iris
Blue Flag Iris (*Iris versicolor*)
   *Also known as flag lily and wild iris

Common Flag Iris (*I. germanica*)
   *Also known as German iris

Florentine Iris (*I. florentina*)

Sweet Flag Iris (*I. pallida*)
   *Also known as Dalmatian iris

---

32   *Ibid.*, 9.

The iris flower has three upright petals called "standards" and three lower petals called "falls." These flowers grow atop stems that reach between two and three feet tall. Some irises have "beards," which are fuzzy areas on the lower/fall petals. The word flag in the common name comes from the Middle English *flagge*, meaning "rush" or "reed" because iris leaves resemble rushes.[33] There are about two hundred species of iris worldwide.

Blue flag is bluish-purple with narrow standards, and falls with yellow veining. The falls have a central yellow area surrounded by white. Common flag has lilac to purple falls with yellow beards and slightly lighter-colored standards. The Florentine iris is white or pale bluish-gray with yellow beards, and sweet flag is lavender-blue with yellow beards.

Orris root is a powder made from the rhizomes of three types of iris: the Florentine, common, and blue flag. This powder is used as a scent fixative for perfumes and potpourris, and has a violet-like aroma. Used in perfumery by the Greeks and Romans, orris root was also used medicinally through the Middle Ages.

Because of their beauty and variety of colors, the genus of this plant was named for the Greek goddess Iris. She was a messenger for the gods and appeared to mortals as a rainbow. Because Iris also guided souls between the worlds, the Greeks associated this flower with the otherworld.

Place a couple of iris flowers on your altar to engender healing energy. Growing them in your garden or placing a vase of cut flowers in a prominent place in your home invites domestic bliss. Place three flowers where you work to act as a muse that will stimulate your creativity. Burn a dried flower in a spell to bring success. Use orris root powder or pieces of dried rhizome from any species of iris in sachets for love magic or as an amulet for protection. Burn a pinch of rhizome to purify an area.

Iris is associated with the element water. Its astrological influence comes from the moon and Venus. This flower is also associated with the following deities: Hera, Horus, Iris, Isis, and Juno.

---

33  Jack Sanders, *Secrets of Wildflowers: A Delightful Feast of Little-Known Facts, Folklore, and History* (Guilford, CT: Globe Pequot Press, 2014), 78.

## Primrose

Common Primrose (*Primula vulgaris* syn. *P. acaulis*)
   *Also known as butter rose, English primrose, and key flower

Polyanthus Primrose (*P.* × *polyantha*)
   *Also known as florists' primrose

Crinkled green leaves form a rosette at the base of these plants. The six-petaled flowers grow in clusters that rise on stems about six inches from the base of the plant. The common primrose flower is pale yellow. The polyanthus primrose encompasses a group of hybrids with flower colors that can be blue, orange, pink, purple, white, or yellow.

The name primrose comes from the Latin *prima rosa*, meaning "first rose."[34] Although they are not related to roses, these early-blooming flowers have a rose-like appearance. And despite the common name, these plants are not related to evening primrose (*Oenothera biennis*).

The name primrose is also a folk name for its cousin the English cowslip (*P. veris*). In the wild the primrose and cowslip hybridize producing the oxlip (*P. elatior*). The polyanthus primrose is a complex hybrid created from the common primrose, the English cowslip, and the oxlip.

For centuries the primrose has been regarded as a magical plant associated with fairies and other nature spirits. According to legends, dryads were said to pick these flowers during the dark of the new moon. In medieval times, primroses were used to flavor mead. In German folklore, the primrose was called key flower and believed to provide entrance to hillsides and caverns. In Norse folklore, Freya used this flower to unlock the seasonal gates of spring.

This plant is associated with lusty Beltane celebrations and fertility. Place a potted primrose on your altar to invoke the Goddess. The primrose and yellow flowers in general are used on May Day to strew across thresholds. Planting them by your front door or strewing the flower petals will invite the fairies to bless your home. Also planting them in the garden will attract fairies and other nature spirits to your property. Place a

---

34   Philip Carr-Gomm and Stephanie Carr-Gomm, *The Druid Plant Oracle: Working with the Magical Flora of the Druid Tradition* (London: Eddison Sadd Editions, Limited, 2007), 94.

couple of flowers on your altar to aid in fairy magic. A sachet of dried flowers and leaves enhances dreams. In addition, carrying a primrose flower attracts love.

Primrose is associated with the elements air, earth, and fire. It is also associated with fairies and the goddesses Bertha and Freya. Its astrological influence comes from Venus.

### Solomon's Seal
(*Polygonatum biflorum*)
  *Also known as lady's seals, sealwort, sealroot, and sow's teats

This plant's single arching stem has lance-shaped leaves with prominent veins. The flowers grow in little drooping clusters that dangle beneath the stem under the leaves. They are tubular in shape, a creamy or waxy white, and topped with yellowish-green.

The genus name *Polygonatum* is Greek meaning "many jointed," referring to the angled joints of the root.[35] Although the species name *biflorum* refers to the flowers, which hang in pairs, there are sometimes more than two together.

The Israelite King Solomon was said to have great wisdom, and to possess a special signet/seal ring that aided him in his magic work. According to herbal lore, he was said to have placed his seal upon this plant when he realized its value. The circular scars on the rootstock, which are said to be his seal, are actually left by the stems that die back after the growing season.

Solomon's seal is effective in repelling negative energy. Plant it in an area of your property where you feel the need for protection for your home and family. Burn a few dried leaves to consecrate ritual space. The dried root can be burned as an incense offering to deities or to bind an oath. Meditating with the root aids in developing inner wisdom.

You can buy Solomon's seal oil or make your own. Make an infusion of the root by cutting it into small pieces, placing them in a jar, and then pouring in enough olive oil to cover the pieces. Put the lid on the jar and gently swirl the contents. Place the jar where it will stay at room temperature for four weeks. If most of the oil gets absorbed

---

35  Inge N. Dobelis, ed., *Magic and Medicine of Plants: A Practical Guide to the Science, History, Folklore, and Everyday Uses of Medicinal Plants* (Pleasantville, NY: The Reader's Digest Association, Inc., 1986), 301.

during this time, add more. Strain the oil into a dark glass bottle for storage. Use it to anoint candles and to consecrate ritual or divination tools.

Solomon's seal is associated with the element water, and its astrological influence comes from Saturn.

## Tulip
Garden Tulip (*Tulipa gesneriana*)
  *Also known as Didier's tulip

This popular tulip is one of about a hundred natural species from which hundreds of cultivars and hybrids have been created. Growing from the base of the plant, the broad, gray-green leaves have a tendency to flop over rather than stand up straight. Its flowers come in a range of pinks, reds, oranges, and yellows, and grow on leafless stems.

The earliest-known cultivation of tulips has been traced to Persia around the year 1050.[36] Tulips were used as a symbol of beauty, perfection, and eternity in Persian poetry. In 1554, these flowers were imported into Vienna from Turkey, and they were an immediate hit.[37] Being very expensive and considered a luxury item, tulips were carefully cultivated and prized like jewels. Because ordinary people could not afford them, there is little folklore about tulips.

In the Middle Ages, herbalist John Gerard (1545–1612) noted that tulips were important for their beauty but had no healing virtues. During the nineteenth century they were considered an aphrodisiac, and in the Victorian language of flowers the tulip was an indication of fame.

For magical purposes, tulips have been used to attract love. Color can be employed for different purposes: pink can help kindle flirting and romance, red for passion, and white for fertility. Place a few pink or red petals in a sachet under your pillow to dream of romance or of your lover. Carry a bulb as an amulet for luck, or place a vase of flowers in your kitchen to invite abundance into your home.

---

36  Ina Baghdiantz McCabe, *A History of Global Consumption: 1500–1800* (New York: Routledge, 2015), 161.

37  Kear, *Flower Wisdom*, 200.

Tulip is associated with the element earth, and its astrological influence comes from Venus.

## In the Wild
### Buttercup
Creeping Buttercup (*Ranunculus repens*)

Meadow Buttercup (*R. acris*)

   \*Also known as tall buttercup

There are many species of buttercups and some have been hybridized for the garden. The most familiar are the wild ones that carpet the countryside in spring. The creeping buttercup is a low-growing plant; however, it can reach almost a foot high in areas that are not mowed. Its leaves are deeply lobed and heavily veined. The meadow buttercup grows from one to three feet tall. Its leaves are similar but have a feathery appearance.

Buttercups have shiny, cup-shaped flowers that are, well, the color of butter. The Latin genus name *Ranunculus* means "little frog," referring to the damp places that frogs and these plants like.[38] The meadow buttercup's species name *acris* means "bitter."[39] This is a reference to how it affects the soil around it and limits the growth of other plants. Although these plants can cause skin irritation, the toxins they contain evaporate as they dry out.

Many of us remember the childhood game of holding a flower under someone's chin to determine whether or not he or she liked butter. The yellow reflection or shine meant they did. This was also used to tell whether or not someone was telling the truth, was jealous, or in love with the person holding the flower.

Associated with the sun and positive thoughts, buttercups can be used in spells to attract abundance. Place a bowl of flowers on your altar to aid in deepening your spiritual commitment and to invite ancient wisdom. Dry several sprigs of flowers and leaves for use in spells to manifest your dreams.

Buttercup's astrological influence comes from the fixed star Procyon.

---

38   *Ibid.*, 120.

39   Sanders, *Secrets of Wildflowers*, 66.

*Plantain*

Broadleaf Plantain (*Plantago major*)

   *Also known as common plantain and dooryard plantain

Narrow-leaf Plantain (*P. lanceolata*)

   *Also known as buckhorn plantain and English plantain

First of all, these plants are not related to the banana of the same name. The two plantains included in this book can be found in lawns, meadows, marginal areas, and along roadsides. Both were used medicinally and brought to North America by European settlers.

Broadleaf plantain has a rosette of wide, ribbed leaves that grow close to the ground. The upright stalk has a long, cylindrical flower spike that can be two to six inches long. The phallic appearance of the flower spike caused the plant to be regarded as an aphrodisiac. As expected, the narrow-leaf plantain has narrow, lance-shaped leaves and a tall, thin stalk that holds a dense flower spike one to two inches long. When I was a child, the name we used for the broadleaf plantain was dog ears.

Although these resilient plants are generally thought of as weeds, plantains were once regarded as magical herbs. The Anglo-Saxons considered them important and sacred. Plantains can be used in charms to enhance magical power. As you gather these plants, state what you want to achieve to set your magical purpose. The root can be dried and carried as an amulet to repel negativity and subdue fears. Placed under the bed, it can ward off bad dreams. All parts of the plant can aid in grounding energy after ritual or magic work.

Plantain is associated with the element earth, and its astrological influence comes from Venus and the fixed star Arcturus.

## In the House

With the weather getting warmer, we can bring the outside in by opening windows and bringing in flowering plants or cut flowers. This is a good time to purify and bless your home, and to clean and rededicate your altar and ritual space. In my opinion, there's no better plant to use for this than sweet woodruff.

### Sweet Woodruff

(*Galium odoratum* syn. *Asperula odorata*)

*Also known as lady's bedstraw and waldmeister

Sweet woodruff grows in clumps with stems eight to fifteen inches tall. Whorls of six to eight leaves grow around the stems. Growing in small clusters, its dainty, white flowers are funnel shaped with petals that splay open at the end. While the flowers seem to have little or no fragrance, they develop a strong, sweet, hay-like scent after they are dried. The scent can linger for several years. The dried leaves smell sweet like freshly mown hay or vanilla.

The name woodruff evolved from wood-rove, which was derived from the French *rovelle*, meaning "wheel."[40] This is in reference to the leaves that resemble the spokes of a wheel as they grow in a circle around the stem. Although it is also called lady's bedstraw, its cousin (*Galium verum*) is more widely known by that name. The name waldmeister means master of the forest.

During the Middle Ages, sweet woodruff was strewn on the ground in public places to deter odors and insects. In churches it was intended to ward off evil and pests. Garlands of sweet woodruff were hung in homes to freshen the air. Also, dried leaves and flowers were placed among linens to scent and protect them against insects.

Because the fragrance of sweet woodruff is stronger when dried or crushed, use it as a strewing herb on a porch, patio, or outdoor ritual area. This will scent the air and dispel negative energy. Also infuse the leaves and/or flowers in water and then sprinkle it around the home to purify and bless it. Burning dried leaves or flowers as incense works, too.

Make a tea with one to two teaspoons of dried leaves in one cup of boiling water. Let it steep for at least ten minutes and then strain. Drink this before bed to foster prophetic dreams. Have a question on your mind before going to sleep, and have paper and pen or a smart phone handy at your bedside to take notes when you wake up.

In Germany, sprigs of sweet woodruff were used to make May wine, which was traditionally served in bowls. Make the wine for May Eve or May Day to attune to the season and celebrate. This herbed wine goes nicely over strawberries. Women who are pregnant or breastfeeding should not use sweet woodruff or May wine.

---

40   Grieve, *A Modern Herbal*, 853.

**May Wine**

1 bottle white wine

1 cup fresh leaves

Pick several sprigs of leaves before the flowers bloom and hang them to dry for about a week. Depending on the humidity level, it may take a little longer. Or, lay the leaves on a baking sheet and dry them in a 250 degree Fahrenheit oven with the door open for about twenty minutes. Place the leaves in a pitcher, decant the wine into it, and let sit for several hours. Strain out the leaves before drinking.

Sweet woodruff is associated with the element fire. Its astrological influence comes from the planet Mars and the fixed star Aldebaran.

# May

The world is awash in color as flowers and fruit trees bloom and fill the air with a pot-pourri of sweet perfume. It is no wonder that May is called the magical month. May is strongly associated with other worlds, and the fairy folk are said to be particularly active. This month is named for Maia, a Roman goddess of fertility.

## On the Calendar

### May 1: Beltane/May Day

Beltane celebrates the union of the Goddess and God, fertility, new life, and resurrection. The most widespread and enduring of Beltane rituals is the dance around the maypole. Symbolically it represents male virility and fertility. Like Samhain, the veil between the worlds is thin at Beltane, and the unseen can be seen.

In medieval England, cutting hawthorn on this day symbolized bringing new life into the world and the start of the growing season. To the Celts, Beltane marked the beginning of the summer half of the year when livestock was moved up to hillside pastures. May first was also called Garland Day because garlands of flowers were hung around the necks of cattle. Garlands were also draped over doorways and windows. Hawthorn trees were believed to have a surge of power while in bloom.

In addition to garlands, small baskets called May baskets were filled with flowers, greenery, and sweets, and then hung on neighbors' doors by children. These baskets were a way to share the creative energy of the season and to keep evil spirits at bay. See the "In the House" section of this chapter for instructions on how to make a May basket.

Any type of flower or greenery can be used on the Beltane altar because their beauty and growth represent the fertility and vitality of this sabbat.

### May 4: Veneration of the Thorn

Thorn trees were regarded as guardians of sacred sites and were used to mark holy wells and springs. On this day, devotees would circle around the well or spring and then make offerings to the thorn trees.

......................
### BLACKTHORN
(*Prunus spinosa*)
   *Also known as blackthorn plum and sloe

This shrubby tree's dark-colored bark and dense, spiny branches are the source of its common name. Flowers with five, creamy-white petals bloom shortly before the leaves appear in early spring, standing in stark contrast to the bark. The leaves are broad and oval with serrated edges. Small, round, and blue-black fruit called sloes ripen in the autumn after the first frost.

Blackthorn and hawthorn were used together for hedges to keep animals out of orchards and gardens. They are still part of many hedgerows. During my pilgrimage in Ireland, I saw blackthorns growing at most of the sacred sites I visited.

In Ireland, blackthorn was used for protection against ghosts and evil spells. However, it was also believed that a tribe of fairies called the Lunantishee served as guardians of these trees. Although blackthorn was popular for walking sticks and other uses, the Lunantishee would inflict bad luck on anyone who cut anything from the tree on May 11 or November 11.

On the old Julian calendar, these would have been the days of Beltane and Samhain. A switch was made from the Julian to the Gregorian calendar to more accurately align the months with the seasons. This required ten days to be dropped during the year in which the switch was made.[41]

In keeping with Irish tradition and to appease any fairies or spirits attached to the blackthorn, avoid taking any cuttings on the current or previous dates for Beltane and Samhain. Instead, leave an offering for the Lunantishee at the base of the tree or in its branches. At other times, ask permission to collect leaves and small branches with thorns. Place the thorns on your altar during spells for protection. Alternatively, place three thorns at each corner of your house as you say:

> *With these thorns that I now place; negativity, be banned from this space.*
> *Protected by the blackthorn tree; this spell be strong, so mote it be.*

Dried leaves can be strewn around an outdoor ritual area for protection as well as to boost magical energy. Instead of using thorns, draw blackthorn's associated ogham or rune on small stones to use in their place. Place one of these stones on your altar on May 4th to honor this legendary fairy tree. Crumble and burn a few leaves to give strength to any type of spell. If you do not have access to a blackthorn tree, carve its ogham or rune into the candles that you use for spells or rituals.

Blackthorn is associated with the elements earth and fire. Its astrological influence comes from Mars and Saturn. In addition to fairies, this tree is associated with the following deities: Banba, Belenus, Bertha, Brigid, the Dagda, Holle, Loki, and Macha.

*Figure 11. Blackthorn is associated with the ogham*
*Straif (left) and the rune Thurisaz (right).*

---

41    Esther Yu Sumner, "A Date is a Date is a Date," *Ancestry Magazine*, Vol. 25, March-April, 2007 (Provo, UT: Ancestry, Inc.), 20.

## *May 13: The Celtic Month of Hawthorn Begins*

Hawthorne is associated with healing and balance, spiritual energies, protection, and most importantly, the fairies. It is the symbol of approaching summer, prosperity, and enchantment.

......................
### HAWTHORN

Common Hawthorn (*Crataegus monogyna*)
  *Also known as one-seeded hawthorn

English Hawthorn (*C. laevigata* syn. *C. oxyacanthoides*)
  *Also known as Midland hawthorn

Both trees are also known as haw, May, and whitethorn

Both of these hawthorns are less than twenty feet tall and have grayish-colored bark. They have shiny, somewhat oval leaves with rounded lobes and thorns that grow along the branches. Five-petaled flowers grow in clusters. The flowers of the common hawthorn are white, often with a pinkish blush; the English hawthorn's flowers have a slight purplish tint. The oval red fruit that ripens in the autumn are called haws.

Hawthorn was commonly called May for the month in which it blooms, and whitethorn, because of its grayish-colored bark. The name hawthorn was derived from the German *hagedorn*, which means "hedge thorn."[42] The genus name *Crataegus* comes from the Greek *kratos*, meaning "strength," which underlines its popularity for making broomsticks.[43] The name one-seeded hawthorn comes from the fact that the fruit contains only one seed.

The ancient Romans considered this tree a symbol of marriage, and both Roman and Greek brides often wore crowns of hawthorn flowers. In addition to being highly praised by poets from Chaucer onwards, the hawthorn is regarded as an important fairy tree in the British Isles. Instead of removing a hawthorn from the middle of a field, farmers plow around the tree rather than disturb the wee folk.

---

42  Grieve, *A Modern Herbal*, 385.

43  Coombes, *Dictionary of Plant Names*, 98.

Like many plants, there is differing folklore about taking the flowers indoors. However, blossoms were taken indoors in Ireland on May Day to protect a house from evil. Another belief was that a broomstick made of hawthorn should not be taken into the home because it would be an indication of death.

As we have seen, hawthorn is closely associated with Beltane, and it was believed to have a surge of power when in bloom. One power that this tree offers is protection. While a belief persisted that it protected against lightning and evil spirits, it is also effective to dispel any form of negativity. Use leaves or flowers for protection spells, or carry one of them in your pocket or purse. Sprinkle petals on the ground just before ritual to cleanse and sanctify the area. The flowers can be used in charms for attracting love, and they add strength to a relationship when included in a handfasting bouquet.

Because this is an important fairy tree, be sure to leave a gift when taking anything from it—even any parts that you find on the ground. Wear a sprig of hawthorn flowers and/or leaves to contact fairies and other nature spirits.

Hawthorn is associated with the elements air and fire. Its astrological influence comes from Mars. This tree is associated with fairies and the following deities: Belenus, Brigid, Danu, the Dagda, Frigg, Thor, and Zeus.

*Figure 12. Hawthorn is associated with the ogham Huath (left) and the rune Othila (right).*

## In the Garden
### Columbine
Garden Columbine (*Aquilegia vulgaris*)
   *Also known as European columbine and granny's bonnet

Wild Columbine (*A. canadensis*)
   *Also known as culverwort and lion's herb

A favored garden flower for centuries, there are now over seventy species of columbine. Drooping, bell-like flowers with distinctive backward-pointing spurs grow on long, branching stalks one to three feet tall. The flowers give way to seeds that look like clusters of small, upright peapods. The wild columbine has red and yellow flowers with long spurs; garden columbine has violet-blue flowers with short spurs. Columbine's medium-green leaves are rounded and lobed.

Herbalists from ancient times through the Middle Ages used columbine for a range of ailments. In addition, young newly married couples were advised to use columbine for protection against witches.

This plant's genus and common names come from Latin with *aquila*, meaning "eagle," and *columba*, "dove."[44] The flower spurs have been likened to an eagle's talons, and groups of flowers are said to resemble a flight of doves. The Saxons called this plant culverwort from their word *culfre*, meaning "pigeon."[45] The name lion's herb comes from a story that young lions ate columbine to increase their strength.

Grown in a garden, columbine brings blessings to the home. Scattering leaves and flowers across the front door threshold combats jealousy. Carrying a dried flower bolsters courage and balances emotions. Columbine's association with the eagle, dove, and pigeon makes it instrumental in working with bird magic. Also use it for ritual or magic work in which balance is important. Infuse seedpods in olive oil and then use the oil to prepare candles for spells to attract love.

Columbine is associated with the element water, and its astrological influence comes from Venus.

### Comfrey
Common Comfrey (*Symphytum officinale*)
   *Also known as ass ear, blackwort, and knitbone

Introduced into North America by early European settlers, comfrey now grows wild in some areas. It has dark green, oval leaves on an erect stem that grows up to three feet tall. Its creamy yellow to purplish, bell-shaped flowers grow in clusters and bloom from May to September. When not in bloom, comfrey can be mistaken for foxglove.

---

44   Frances Tenenbaum, ed., *Taylor's Encyclopedia of Garden Plants* (New York: Houghton Mifflin Company, 2003), 31.

45   Grieve, *A Modern Herbal*, 214.

The Greeks and Romans considered this plant a master healer and used it for a wide range of ailments. In the Middle Ages it was attributed with healing broken bones. Its genus name comes from the Greek *symphyo*, meaning "grown together" or "to unite," referring to its mending properties.[46] The name comfrey was derived from the Latin *conferva*, meaning "knitting together."[47] Despite its reputation in the past, current opinions differ on comfrey's safety when taken internally.

Wear or carry a leaf for safe and easy travel. In addition, a piece of comfrey root in your suitcase is said to aid its safe arrival at your destination. Place a piece of dried root in your pocket for protection when traveling in the astral realm. Use crumbled, dried leaves and/or flowers to strew around your property to invite blessings and attract abundance. Planting comfrey in several places around the garden will bring stability to your household. Burn small pieces of dried root to boost the energy of spells that banish or bind. To enhance psychic abilities, place four dried leaves in the cardinal directions on your altar.

Comfrey is associated with the elements air, earth, and water. Its astrological influence comes from the planet Saturn and the fixed star Ala Corvi.

### Lilac
Common Lilac (*Syringa vulgaris*)
  *Also known as French lilac

Lilac is a multi-stemmed shrub that reaches twelve to fifteen feet tall and can spread eight to twelve feet across. It is widely loved for its fragrant flowers that bloom in April and May. The four-lobed, tubular flowers grow in large, hanging, pyramidal clusters. They range from white to lilac to purple. The pointed, heart-shaped leaves are gray-green or blue-green. The delightful fragrance of lilacs is so popular that many arboretums have a special event called lilac Sunday so people can enjoy them in full bloom.

Lilac's genus name comes from the Greek word *syrinx* meaning tube or pipe. *Syringa* was originally applied to what is now the *Philadelphus* genus of mock orange because of

---

46  *Ibid.*, 215.
47  Dobelis, *Magic and Medicine of Plants*, 147.

its pipe-like stems. At that time the mock orange shrub and lilac were classified together. However, in the seventeenth century when these plants were separated into their own genera, the name *Syringa* stayed with the lilac.[48]

According to folklore in England, white lilacs were considered unlucky to wear except on May Day. If a lilac bush was cut down, it was believed that other lilacs in the area would mourn and not produce flowers the following year. Other folklore indicated that the lilac was used for weather divination. If the blossoms faded quickly, the summer would be warm; if it flowered late, the summer season would be rainy.

Although it was once customary to plant lilacs in front of a house, growing it anywhere on your property will invite nature spirits and fairies to take up residence. Place a vase of fresh-cut flowers by your bed to enhance dream work and foster prophetic dreams. The scent of lilacs also aids divination, clairvoyance, and helps in accessing past-life memories. Place flowers on your desk or workspace to increase creativity. Fresh flowers on your altar enhance an esbat ritual or any lunar workings. Fresh or dried flowers are effective in spells to attract love. Dried leaves and flowers can be burned for defensive magic and to break hexes. In addition to repelling negative energy, the smoke aids in banishing unwanted spirits.

Lilac is associated with the element water and with fairies. Its astrological influence comes from Mercury, the moon, and Venus.

*Figure 13. Lilac is associated with the rune Eihwaz.*

### Lily of the Valley
(*Convallaria majalis*)
   *Also known as fairy ladder, ladder to heaven, May bells, and May lily

---

48   Joan Parry Dutton, *Plants of Colonial Williamsburg: How to Identify 200 of Colonial America's Flowers, Herbs, and Trees* (Williamsburg, VA: The Colonial Williamsburg Foundation, 1994), 69.

This tiny flower is famous for its powerful scent. Blooming for most of the month of May, these white, bell-shaped flowers are suspended in a row from arching stems. The leaves are wide and lance shaped. Only six to nine inches tall, this plant can be invasive and needs to be kept in check.

The species name, *majalis*, means "of the month of May."[49] Lily of the valley is a symbol of May Day and associated with fairies. Often grown in graveyards, it was given the folk name ladder to heaven. According to one legend, these flowers were created from the drops of dragon blood that spilled on the ground when it was slain by Saint Louis of France.

Medicinal use of lily of the valley dates back to ancient Greece, and in the Middle Ages it was believed to be an aid for memory. In the Victorian language of flowers, it signified that happiness would return.

Include lily of the valley on your Beltane altar, and keep a bouquet on hand for magic work. Grown in the garden, these flowers will attract happiness into your home. On Beltane, leave an offering for fairies under the lily of the valley in your garden. Use dried flowers in spells to heal any rift with a lover or friend. Crumble the dried flowers into your cauldron as you say:

*Sweet scented flower, small as a bee; return this person close to me. Heal the feelings that pulled us apart; help us gain a fresh, new start.*

Also dry some of the rhizomes and grind them into a powder. Add a pinch of the powder to incense for fostering success and reaching your goals.

Lily of the valley is associated with the element air. It is also associated with fairies and the gods Apollo and Asclepius. This plant's astrological influence comes from Mercury.

*Figure 14. Lily of the Valley is associated with the rune Hagalaz.*

---

49   Lucia Impelluso, *Nature and Its Symbols*, translated by Stephen Sartarelli (Los Angeles: Getty Publications, 2004), 79.

### Rosemary
(*Rosmarinus officinalis*)
　　*Also known as elf leaf, rosmarine, and sea dew

Often growing on sea cliffs around the Mediterranean, rosemary was described as having the smell of the ocean with a hint of pine. This is the source of its genus name, which means "dew of the sea."[50] Rosemary is a shrubby evergreen perennial that often reaches six feet in height. It has short, stiff, needle-like leaves similar to spruce trees. Its pale blue, tubular-shaped flowers grow in clusters of two or three. They bloom from late winter to early spring and sometimes intermittently throughout the year.

Since ancient times, rosemary was used in religious ceremonies, magic spells, and more mundanely as a medicinal herb. The Greeks and Romans used it at weddings as a symbol of fidelity and at funerals for remembrance. In the belief that rosemary improved memory, students in ancient Greece burned it or wore a sprig of it in their hair for help in passing exams. The folk name elf leaf is in reference to the belief that these magical beings lived among the rosemary bushes.

Rosemary's cleansing properties make it useful for clearing negativity. Burn a few dried leaves before ritual, magic, or healing work. Also burn it for defensive magic to release and protect against hexes. Using it in food to reduce the intensity of strong emotions makes it helpful in balancing relationships and engendering fidelity between lovers. Also use dried leaves and/or flowers in spells to bind people together. While it can attract elves and fairies, it also protects against malicious entities. Rosemary enhances awareness and increases magic and psychic powers.

Rosemary is associated with the element fire and with fairies and elves. Its astrological influence comes from the planet Mercury, the moon, the sun, and the fixed star Alphecca.

*Figure 15. Rosemary is associated with the rune Jera.*

---

50　Coombes, *Dictionary of Plant Names*, 173.

## *Valerian*

Common Valerian (*Valeriana officinalis*)

> *Also known as all-heal, cat valerian, garden heliotrope, and vandalroot

Reaching three to five feet tall, valerian has round, erect stems and dark green, toothed leaves. The small, five-petaled flowers are white with a tinge of pink, but they can be more pink or even lavender. The flowers grow in dense clusters and bloom from late spring through early to midsummer. The pale brown, clustered root is an upright rhizome with fibrous roots extending outward.

Valerian's common name is thought to have come from the Latin *valere*, meaning "to be well."[51] During the Middle Ages, it was known as all-heal, referring to its range of medicinal applications. The name vandalroot comes from the Swedish *Vändelrot*, a reference to its use by Teutonic tribes known as the Vandals.[52] Although the names seem similar, Valium does not come from valerian.

Rodents are attracted to this herb, and it is believed that the Pied Piper of Hamelin used valerian to lure the rats away from the city. Also, cats actually love valerian as much as catnip. While the flowers have a sweet, cherry-vanilla fragrance, it is usually overwhelmed by the odor of the leaves and stems, which have been described as smelling like dirty socks.

Valerian is powerful for purification purposes. Make a maceration by chopping about an ounce of fresh roots into small pieces. Place them in a jar and then pour a pint of cold water over them. Let the roots soak for eight to ten hours. Strain out the pieces, and then use the water to consecrate new ritual tools as well as ritual space.

A piece of dried root can be used as a love amulet. It also aids in healing quarrels between lovers. The flowers can be used to support love and money spells.

---

51   Chevallier, *The Encyclopedia of Medicinal Plants*, 146.

52   Arthur O. Tucker and Thomas DeBaggio, *The Encyclopedia of Herbs: A Comprehensive Reference to Herbs and Flavor and Fragrance* (Portland, OR: Timber Press, Inc., 2009), 498.

Use dried leaves to aid in breaking hexes. Hang a sprig of flowers and/or leaves over an exterior door to protect the home.

Valerian is associated with the element water and the goddess Epona. Its astrological influence comes from Mercury and Venus.

### Yarrow

Common Yarrow (*Achillea millefolium*)
> *Also known as bloodwort, devil's plaything, milfoil,
> and thousand leaf

Yarrow is a slender, upright plant that grows one to three feet tall with branching stems. Its leaves are fern-like and covered with soft hairs. Small, white to pinkish colored flowers grow in wide umbel clusters and bloom from midsummer to autumn. The plant has a pleasant, sweet-herby smell.

To the Greeks, yarrow was an important medicinal herb that was named in honor of the hero Achilles, who was said to have used it to heal the wounds of his fellow soldiers at the battle of Troy. In the past, yarrow was prescribed for just about every ailment. In addition, the ancient Chinese used yarrow stems as *I Ching* divination sticks. The folk name devil's plaything came from the belief that Satan used yarrow to cast spells.

According to folklore, young women were told to pick yarrow flowers by moonlight for love divination. If dewdrops were still on them in the morning, a woman's favorite man would propose marriage.

Yarrow's grounding energy clears away negativity, releases hexes, and banishes anything unwanted from your home or life. Use it to purify ritual space by scattering leaves or flowers on your altar or on the floor. Consecrate magic and ritual tools by storing yarrow flowers with them. A bouquet of fresh flowers or a bowl of dried ones aids in stimulating intuition and psychic abilities for divination. Wrap several leaves and/or flowers in a soft cloth and place them under your pillow for dream work.

Yarrow is associated with the elements air and water. Its astrological influence comes from Venus. This plant is also associated with the god Cernunnos.

## In the Wild

### *Cinquefoil*

Creeping Cinquefoil (*Potentilla reptans*)

   *Also known as European cinquefoil

Dwarf Cinquefoil (*P. canadensis*)

Creeping cinquefoil grows four to six inches tall and has yellow, five-petaled flowers that resemble small, wild roses. Stalks with a single flower or leaf rise up from the stems, which grow along the ground. Leaves consist of five or seven oval, coarsely toothed leaflets. Dwarf cinquefoil is two to four inches tall and has similar flowers. Its leaflets are wedge shaped. The leaves on both of these plants grow in a circular pattern around the stalks. Their flowers bloom from May to August.

The genus name *Potentilla* comes from the Latin *potens*, which means "powerful."[53] For this reason, medieval knights often used the leaf as an emblem on their shields. The name cinquefoil means "five leaves."[54] Cinquefoil has been associated with mothers and their children because the leaves bend over and shield the flowers when it rains.

While this plant was, according to legend, used for protection against witches, it was also believed that witches rubbed it on their bodies to produce a trancelike state. Cinquefoil was said to be one of the few yellow flowers acceptable to Hecate for her garden.

Hang a sprig of leaves over your front door for protection. A flower and sprig of leaves in a sachet can be used as a charm to strengthen the relationship with your mother and/or child.

To break a hex or any form of negative magic, make an infusion of leaves. Without straining out the plant material, take it outside and pour it on the ground as you say:

*This spell that someone tried to cast; is not to be, it will not last. With this potion I now pour; all harm is banished from my door.*

---

53   Coombes, *Dictionary of Plant Names*, 161.

54   Barbara Medina and Victor Medina, *Central Appalachian Wildflowers* (Guilford, CT: The Globe Pequot Press, 2002), 102.

Other cinquefoils often mentioned for magic work include silverweed cinquefoil (*Potentilla anserina* syn. *Argentina anserina*), which is also known as common silverweed. This plant can be distinguished by its numerous leaflets along the stems rather than in a circle around them. Shrubby cinquefoil (*Potentilla fruticosa* syn. *Dasiphora fruticosa*) is a bushy shrub that grows about three feet tall.

Cinquefoil is associated with the elements earth and fire. Its astrological influence comes from Jupiter and Mercury.

## In the House
### *How to Make a May Basket*
Making May baskets is a wonderful children's activity that's fun for adults, too. However, don't feel limited to making them only on May Day. Using these little baskets throughout the summer months is a great way to enjoy the scent of flowers and herbs.

To make a May basket, take a piece of 8½ × 11 construction paper. Gently fold a short side over so it is flush with a long side of the paper, and then cut off the excess strip along the top. Now a perfect square, hold the paper at an angle so one corner points up, one points down, and the other two point right and left. Bring the two side corners together creating a cone. Staple the bottom and the top edges together. The other part of this seam can be taped together from inside the basket. The opposite side of the cone is higher and creates a nice backdrop for the flowers and herbs that will be inserted into the basket.

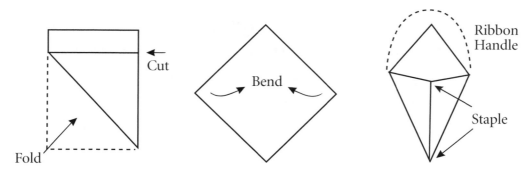

*Figure 16. Follow these steps to make a May basket.*

The basket can be decorated with sequins, pieces of ribbon, lace, or anything. If you use a dark-colored paper, attach a white, lacy paper doily to the outside to decorate it. Alternatively, leftover pieces of wallpaper can be used instead of construction paper.

To finish the basket, staple a sturdy wide ribbon above the opening for a handle. Collect flowers and sprigs of herbs to put in the basket, and then hang it on a doorknob.

### Dreaming of Flowers

At this time of year, dreams that include flowers are thought to be more potent and have special significance. Keep a journal or smart phone at your bedside to record your dreams. Table 5 lists the meanings for some of the flowers that may appear in dreams.

| Table 5. Flower Meanings in Dreams | |
|---|---|
| Asters | Happiness and abundance |
| Azaleas | An unexpected gift |
| Bluebells | True love |
| Buttercup | Improved business prospects |
| Columbine | Happy adventure |
| Cowslip | Unexpected good luck |
| Crocus | A new start |
| Daffodil | Love and happiness is coming |
| Daisies | A birth, heading for success |
| Dandelion | Happiness in love |
| Foxglove | Luck in love |

| Table 5. Flower Meanings in Dreams (continued) | |
|---|---|
| Geranium | Considerable wealth |
| Honeysuckle | A move to a better house |
| Iris | Good news |
| Jasmine | Achieve high ambitions |
| Lavender | A reunion, plenty of money |
| Lily | Seek solitude |
| Lotus | Peace |
| Marigold | You will do well in life |
| Orange blossom | Marriage |
| Pansy | Contentment |
| Primrose | New friendship |
| Rose | Love will soon enter your life |
| Tulip | Joy, good luck, a marriage proposal |
| Violet | Success and happiness |
| Wallflower | Pleasure and contentment |

# June

This is a month filled with sunlight and long days. Before the high heat arrives, there is a brief period of time to enjoy the soft side of summer. Tending a garden or taking a long walk in nature helps us tune into the rhythms of the green world when life is at its fullest. The month of June was named for the Roman goddess Juno. Because she was considered a goddess of marriage, June became a popular month in which to tie the knot or jump the broomstick.

## On the Calendar
### June 10: The Celtic Month of Oak Begins
Oaks live for many centuries and are bound up with human history. They were considered especially sacred to the Greeks and Romans, who associated them with their most powerful gods. In the British Isles, the Celtic god Bilé and the Druids are very closely linked with this tree. According to legend, King Arthur's roundtable was made from oak, and Sherwood Forest with its massive Major Oak is linked with Robin Hood.

........

## Oak

Black Oak (*Quercus velutina*)

White Oak (*Q. alba*)

These two types of oak trees are some of the most common in North America. The black oak's leaves have pointed lobes tipped with tiny bristles. The white oak's are rounded and smooth. The acorns of the black oak take two years to mature; the white oak's acorns mature in one year.

The genus name *Quercus* comes from the Celtic *quer*, meaning "fine," and *cuez*, "tree."[55] This is quite fitting, as oaks are very large, stately trees that exude powerful energy. While fresh acorns won't be available until late summer or early autumn, leaves and bark are just as effective for magic work and ritual.

Oak leaves in the home help clear away negative energy, and when used on the altar in ritual they represent the potency of the God. For healing and seeking wisdom, hold a piece of bark between your hands and visualize your desired outcome. Also use a piece of bark to help ground energy after ritual. Dry a small twig with leaves and hang it in your kitchen to invite abundance into your home. Leaves placed under the bed aids fertility and virility. To add power to spells, make a cross by tying two bare twigs together with black thread, which will draw elemental balance along with the strength of the oak. In addition, the associated ogham or runes can be carved into a brown candle to represent the oak.

Oak is associated with the elements air, earth, and fire. Its astrological influence comes from Jupiter and the sun. This tree is associated with the Green Man and the following deities: Artemis, Apollo, Ares, Balder, Bilé, Brigid, Ceres, Cernunnos, Cerridwen, Cybele, the Dagda, Demeter, Diana, Dôn, Hades, Helios, Hera, Jupiter, Mars, the Morrigan, Odin, Pan, Perun, Pluto, Rhea, Thor, and Zeus.

*Figure 17. Oak is associated with the ogham Duir and the runes Ehwaz, Jera, Raido, Thurisaz, and Teiwaz (shown left to right).*

---

55  Walter P. Wright, *An Encyclopaedia of Gardening* (Bremen, Germany: Salzwasser-Verlag, 2010), 269.

### June 21/22: Summer Solstice/Litha

Summer Solstice falls midway between the two equinoxes. This sabbat is also referred to as Litha from the Anglo-Saxon phrase *Aerra Litha*, which means "before midsummer."[56] This solstice marks the longest day of the year when the sun reaches its farthest point north. Litha is a celebration of the Goddess in full motherhood and the God who is at his pinnacle of power. Herbs and flowers gathered at this time were considered particularly potent.

Place flowers and sun symbols on your solstice altar. To symbolize the vitality of the Green Man, include oak leaves. The oak tree shares the dual kingship of the green world with holly. Representing the light and dark halves of the year, the oak king and holly king trade places at the solstices. Although the Celtic tree month of oak has just begun, this is the solstice when the holly king begins his reign. Even though there are many long, bright summer days ahead, the sun begins its journey away from the Northern Hemisphere.

### June 23: Midsummer's Eve

Up until the eighteenth century in rural England, it was customary to light bonfires on hilltops on this night to celebrate the long summer days. When the fires died down, people would leap over them for the symbolic purification of smoke. Because witches and fairies were believed to be particularly active on this night, bundles of Saint John's wort and rowan were tied with ribbon and tossed onto the bonfire to raise protective energy. Garlands of Saint John's wort, plantain, and yarrow were also burned for protection against evil spirits. In place of bonfires, lamps were placed in windows surrounded by flowers and kept lit all night.

### June 24: Midsummer's Day

Midsummer's Day was a major festival day to celebrate the abundance and mystery of nature. One form of divination on this day was for a woman to pick a handful of grass with her eyes closed. The number of daisies pulled up with the grass indicated

---

56 Diane Ferguson, *The Magickal Year: A Pagan Perspective on the Natural World* (New York: Labyrinth Books, 1996), 144.

the number of years before marriage, or if she was married, the number of children she would have.

In another form of love divination, a flower of Saint John's wort was plucked on Midsummer's Eve and if it was still fresh and not wilted in the morning, marriage prospects were good. In addition, this was considered a good time to dowse for water. Midsummer also marked the time of year when Druids performed the fabled rite of cutting mistletoe when it was at its height of vigorous growth.

Under the category of "if you can't beat them, join them," the feast of Saint John was a Christian substitute for the celebrations that were centered on this time of year. The counterparts to Saint John's Day and summer solstice are Christmas and the winter solstice. In essence, Jesus and Saint John took the place of the oak and holly kings.

..................................

## Saint John's Wort
(*Hypericum perforatum*)
 *Also known as chase-devil and rosin rose

Saint John's wort is a shrubby plant that reaches two to three feet in height, and has pale green, oblong leaves. Bright yellow, star-shaped flowers grow in clusters at the ends of branches and have a light, lemon-like scent. You may find several types of Saint John's wort at garden centers, but *Hypericum perforatum* is the one that is used medicinally.

This plant has a long history in medicine and magic that dates back to the ancient Greeks and Romans. In Christian times it was named Saint John's wort because it blooms around the time of the saint's feast day. The name rosin rose comes from a characteristic of the flowers and buds: when they are squeezed or bruised they ooze a red liquid that looks like rosin."

Traditionally, a sprig of Saint John's wort was hung above a doorway to protect a house from evil and lightning. The name chase-devil comes from the belief that it could ward off evil and prevent attacks from demons. During the Middle Ages, monks used this plant for exorcisms. It is thought that the attribute of chasing away evil spirits or demons from a person may have come from the plant's ability to alleviate depression.

Grow Saint John's wort near your front door or hang a sprig over it to repel negativity and invite abundance into your home. Burn dried leaves in a fireplace or cauldron and let its pungent smoke purify your house and/or ritual area. Burning the leaves also prevents enchantments. Use the flowers in love charms and spells to aid fertility.

Saint John's wort is associated with the element fire and the god Balder. Its astrological influence comes from the sun.

## In the Garden
### Elder
Common Elder (*Sambucus canadensis*)
    *Also known as American elderberry

Black Elder (*S. nigra*)
    *Also known as European elder, lady elder, and a plethora
     of other names

Growing five to twelve feet tall and wide, the common elder is a garden plant that is also found in fields and meadows. The European elder can reach eight to twenty feet tall and wide. Both elders have oval, toothed leaves. Their small white flowers grow in large flattened clusters that can be ten inches wide. The flowers give way to clusters of round, bluish-black berries that ripen in late summer or early autumn. The common elder flowers have a lemon-like scent, while the black elder flowers smell musky.

The roots, stems, and leaves of elder are toxic. Although tart, the ripe, cooked berries are edible and often used to make jam and wine. Elderberries have a long history of use and have been found in excavations of Stone Age sites. Elderflowers are also edible and used for tea as well as to make wine.

In Denmark it was believed that standing under an elder on Midsummer's Eve allowed a person to see the fairy king and his entourage. Likewise in England, adding elderflowers to the Midsummer's Eve bonfire allowed people to see fairies and nature devas. Growing elder in the garden invites fairies and nature spirits, who are said to like swinging and playing in the branches.

Combine elderflowers and Saint John's wort flowers to add power to spells. If you are concerned about hexes or dark magic, hang elderflowers over your altar. As you do this, say three times:

*Lady Elder, powerful tree; I call to you, please aid me. Keep at bay, those who may do harm; make these flowers a powerful charm.*

Elderflowers can be used as an offering in ritual, and sprinkling an infusion cleanses an area before ritual or magic work. Associated with death and funerals, burying elderflowers with the deceased or sprinkling them on the grave aids a loved one's passage into the otherworld.

Elder is associated with all the elements but especially water. Its astrological influence comes from Mercury and Venus. This tree is associated with fairies, and the following deities: Bertha, Boann, Cailleach Bheur, the Dagda, Danu, Freya, Freyr, Gaia, Holle, Rhea, Venus, and Vulcan.

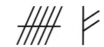

*Figure 18. Elder is associated with the ogham Ruis (left) and the rune Fehu (right).*

## Foxglove
Common Foxglove (*Digitalis purpurea*)
   *Also known as fairy caps, folks glove, fox bells, purple foxglove, and witches' bells

Foxglove is a beloved garden plant with downward-pointing, tubular, bell-shaped flowers that are usually purplish-pink or white. The oval leaves are soft and hairy. In its first year, the plant only consists of a rosette of leaves. The second year of growth produces tall spires of flowers that reach three to five feet high. This famous flower is lovely but dangerous. All parts of the plant are poisonous if eaten and contact may cause skin irritation.

While there are many theories for the "fox" in the name foxglove, the most agreed upon one is that it is a corruption of the name folk's glove. This is a reference to the fairy folk wearing the flowers as gloves. The genus name *digitalis* is from the Latin *digitabulum*, meaning "thimble" or a sort of finger protection.[57] Its use for treating heart

---

57   Grieve, *A Modern Herbal*, 323.

ailments came to the attention of English physician William Withering in 1775 from an old wise woman healer.[58] Perhaps the fairies are at work because despite many attempts, scientists have not been able to duplicate *digitalis* in the laboratory.

According to folklore, flower spires bending over are a sign that fairies or pixies are inside the blossoms. Also, the spots on the interior of the flowers were said to be where elves touched them.

As long as you have an open heart, foxglove can help you befriend the fairies or other nature spirits that may be living in your garden. Without removing a leaf from the plant, hold it between your hands and whisper a greeting to them. Listen very carefully for a response but don't be disappointed if you do not hear one. Fairies make contact when they are ready. Leave an offering for them under the plant.

Foxglove is associated with the element water and with fairies. Its astrological influence comes from Venus.

### Lady's Mantle

Common Lady's Mantle (*Alchemilla vulgaris*)

Soft Lady's Mantle (*A. mollis*)

   *Also known as smooth lady's mantle

Both are also known as dew cup and lion's foot

The leaves of these plants are slightly cupped and round with pleated lobes. They are distinctive for their ability to hold beads of rain or dew. Lady's mantle grows in spreading mounds that can be a foot or more wide. Clusters of small flowers bloom from June to August.

A popular garden perennial, soft lady's mantle has gray-green leaves with tiny hairs, which give them a soft texture. This is the source of its species name *mollis*, which means "soft."[59] Its flowers are yellowish-green and grow atop stems that are about eighteen inches tall. Common lady's mantle has fewer hairs on its leaves and green flowers. It is a

---

58    Dobelis, *Magic and Medicine of Plants*, 188.

59    Lorraine Harrison, *Latin for Gardeners: Over 3,000 Plant Names Explained and Explored* (Chicago: University of Chicago Press, 2012), 65.

smaller plant with stems reaching only about twelve to fifteen inches tall. Because these two plants are so similar, there is confusion and disagreement as to whether they are actually the same species.

Lady's mantle is called dew cup because moisture remains on its leaves long after evaporating from other plants. Dew was thought to be magical, and lady's mantle was believed to impart even more power to it. Considered the purest form of water, dew was important in alchemy and from this came the genus name *Alchemilla*, which means "little alchemist."[60] Lady's mantle has been used as a medicinal herb for centuries, especially for women's health.

Place a bouquet of flowers on your altar for women's rituals, full moon rituals, and for healing circles. Use dried flowers and/or leaves in sachets for love spells and to increase romance. This plant also boosts the power of other spells. Hold a leaf between your hands to help you focus your mind and energy before divination sessions.

Lady's mantle is associated with the element water and the goddesses Gaia, Demeter, Freya, and Rhea. Its astrological influence comes from Venus.

*Figure 19. Lady's Mantle is associated with the rune Berkana.*

### Mint
Peppermint (*Mentha* × *piperita*)
   *Also known as balm mint and brandy mint

Spearmint (*M. spicata* syn. *M. viridis*)
   *Also known as green mint, lamb mint, our lady's mint,
   and sage of Bethlehem

As members of the mint family, these plants have the distinctive feature of square stems. Peppermint reaches twelve to thirty-six inches in height. Its dark-green leaves are

---

60   Matthew Wood, *The Earthwise Herbal Wisdom: Using Plants as Medicine* (Berkeley, CA: North Atlantic Books, 1997), 65.

deeply veined and toothed. Tiny purple, pink, or white flowers grow in whorls at the tops of the stems. Spearmint has tight whorls of pink or lilac-colored flowers atop spikes of bright-green leaves. Like peppermint, its leaves are deeply veined and toothed. It reaches twelve to eighteen inches tall. Both mints have been used for healing since ancient times.

As previously mentioned, peppermint is a naturally occurring hybrid between spearmint and water mint (*M. aquatica*). Its species name comes from the Latin *piper*, meaning "pepper," because the taste of this herb has a hint of pepper.[61] While spearmint is considered the oldest species of mint, peppermint has been around for quite a long time, too. Dried peppermint leaves have been found in ancient Egyptian burials.

Mint was associated with Demeter who, according to legend, ate a mixture of mint, flour, and water before pursuing Persephone into the underworld. According to legend, this mixture was used during the ancient Mysteries of Demeter rituals at Eleusis. The genus name for mint comes from the nymph Menthe, who transformed herself into a plant to avoid the amorous advances of Hades.

Drink a cup of peppermint tea to help increase psychic awareness, strengthen divination skills, and enhance prophetic dreaming. Use the leaves to activate spells for attracting money, luck, and love. Make spearmint tea and use it to purify ritual objects or drink it to increase spiritual awareness. Place a few spearmint leaves under the front door mat; its protective powers are especially useful for the home because it fosters security. Wrap a stem of peppermint and spearmint together to use as an amulet for attracting prosperity.

The mints are associated with the elements air and fire. The astrological influence for peppermint comes from Mercury, and Spearmint's comes from Venus. Both mints are influenced by the fixed star Capella. These plants are associated with the deities Demeter, Hades, Pluto, and Zeus.

---

61   Jeanne Rose, *375 Essential Oils and Hydrosols* (Berkeley, CA: Frog, Ltd., 1999), 21.

### Mullein

Common Mullein (*Verbascum thapsus*)

  *Also known as flannel leaf, great mullein, Jupiter's staff,
   velvet plant, and witches' candle

Dark Mullein (*V. nigrum*)

  *Also known as black mullein

Mullein (rhymes with sullen) is a biennial plant and, like foxglove, it only has a rosette of leaves in the first year. The large, blue-green leaves are oval shaped and feel like velvet. The spire of flowers that can reach ten feet tall develops in the second year. The yellow, five-petaled flowers have orange stamens and bloom a few at a time from June to September. European settlers unintentionally introduced it into North America.

Dark mullein is a smaller plant with spires only reaching forty inches tall. Its yellow flowers have purple stamens. It, too, was unintentionally introduced into North America.

The common name mullein was derived from the Latin *mollis*, meaning "soft," and its genus name *Verbascum* is a corruption of the Latin *barbascum*, which means "with beard."[62] Both of these names are in reference to the plant's fuzzy texture as are its other names flannel leaf and velvet plant

The Greeks used mullein in medicine and cosmetics. Romans dried the flower spires, dipped them in tallow, and used them as torches. Paradoxically, mullein torches were believed to repel witches, even though it was also believed that witches used them to light their rituals.

Grow at least one mullein plant on your property for protection. Alternatively, grow one at each corner of your property to create the corners of an energy fence. Crumble a dried leaf and burn it in your cauldron to remove negativity from your home. This also protects against hexes. Burning a leaf while meditating helps to connect with ancient wisdom. A sachet of dried leaves or flowers placed under the pillow aids in banishing nightmares. Fresh flowers are effective for love spells.

---

62   Martin, *Wildflower Folklore*, 189.

Cut down a flower spire at the end of the season and let it dry out. Make any needed adjustments to the length so it can serve as a walking stick that will provide magical protection as you ramble through woods or across fields.

Mullein is associated with the element fire and the god Jupiter. Its astrological influence comes from Saturn.

### Strawberry

Garden Strawberry (*Fragaria × ananassa*)

Wild Strawberry (*F. vesca*)

The strawberry plant has short, woody stems and a base rosette of leaves from which rooting runners grow horizontally and form new plants. The leaves are comprised of three toothed leaflets and grow on individual stems. The white, five-petaled flowers grow on separate stems. Botanically, what we consider the seeds are the actual fruits. Growing six inches high, the garden strawberry is a cultivated hybrid of several wild species. The wild strawberry looks like a smaller version of the garden plant. It can be found on moist ground in fields, meadows, and along the edge of woods.

Synonymous with summertime, strawberries are perfect for celebrating the arrival of this season. Even one of the names for this month's full moon is the strawberry moon. Strawberries were valued more for medicinal purposes than culinary use by the ancient Romans. However, by the Middle Ages the French were happily eating them, and in London strawberries were prized treats sold by street vendors.

To stimulate love interest, write your intended's name on a red candle. Place it on your altar along with several strawberries. Light the candle and slowly eat the fruit. Close your eyes and visualize making love with that person to help engender amorous thoughts toward you. Strawberries can also be used to bring harmony, kindle friendship, and support divination.

For a good luck spell, write what you desire on a piece of paper and sprinkle crumbled, dried strawberry leaves on it. Fold up the paper and hold it between your hands as you visualize what you want. When an image is clear, burn the paper and leaves in your cauldron or other safe place. When cool, sprinkle the ashes outside.

Strawberry is associated with the element water and the goddesses Freya, Frigg, and Venus. Its astrological influence comes from Venus.

## In the Wild
### Belladonna
(*Atropa belladonna*)

> *Also known as banewort, deadly nightshade, devil's cherry,
> and witch's berry

Reaching three to five feet tall, belladonna is a shrubby plant with spreading stems. Its broad, oval leaves are dark green, and its elongated, bell-shaped flowers are reddish-purple. Glossy, black berries, about the size of cherries, form from the flowers. Belladonna is found in woods and wastelands. Although extracts from the plant are still used in commercial medicines, it is too deadly for home herbal use because of the fine line between a medicinal and fatal dose.

Belladonna has a dark history stretching back to the ancient Romans, who reputedly used it to poison enemies. There is a plethora of legends about the plant belonging to the devil and about sorcerers and witches who were said to use it in potions that enabled them to fly.

The genus name comes from Atropos, who in Greek mythology was one of the Fates with the power of life and death. The plant's common name comes from sixteenth-century Italy, where it was called *herba bella donna*, "herb of the fair lady," in reference to a practice in which women used juice from the plant to dilate their pupils.[63] While this gave their eyes an effect that was fashionable at the time, it was a practice through which they unintentionally poisoned themselves. If you find belladonna in the wild, leave an offering to Hecate beside it.

Belladonna is associated with the element water and the goddesses Circe, Hecate, and Macha. Its astrological influence comes from Pluto and Saturn.

---

63   Steven Foster and Rebecca L. Johnson, *National Geographic Desk Reference to Nature's Medicine* (Washington, DC: National Geographic Society, 2008), 37.

## Meadowsweet

(*Filipendula ulmaria* syn. *Spiraea ulmaria*)
  *Also known as bridewort, meadwort, and queen of the meadow

Meadowsweet can grow four to six feet tall. The leaves are comprised of oval, toothed leaflets with prominent veins and whitish down on their undersides. Its tiny, five-petaled flowers are creamy white and grow in clusters. They bloom from June through August and have an almond-like scent. Meadowsweet was introduced into North America from Europe.

Meadowsweet's species name means "elm-like," in reference to the shape of its leaves.[64] Its common name is a corruption of meadsweet, which comes from its use as a flavoring for mead. Found in drinking cups that date back to the Neolithic (New Stone Age), traces of meadowsweet attest to its use in brewing for thousands of years. Its use as a medicinal herb continues today.

Use meadowsweet flowers to encourage love and to foster a successful marriage. Scatter fresh-cut meadowsweet as a strewing herb at handfasting rituals. Also include the flowers in a bridal bouquet for blessings of the Goddess. Used around the home, meadowsweet will help bring harmony. Make an infusion for a pre-ritual bath, or use dried flowers to scent ritual clothing.

Meadowsweet is associated with the elements air and water. Its astrological influence comes from Jupiter. This plant is also associated with the goddesses Aine and Danu.

## Vervain

(*Verbena officinalis*)
  *Also known as common verbena, Druid's weed, enchanter's plant,
    simpler's joy, and verbena

Vervain is a sprawling, branching plant that can grow one to three feet tall and wide. The deeply lobed leaves are heavily veined and toothed. Small lavender or pinkish flowers grow on upward-curving stems. The flowers are unscented. Introduced into North America by early settlers, vervain can be found along roadsides, in pastures, and in wastelands.

---

64   Grieve, *A Modern Herbal*, 524.

Although this is an unassuming plant, the Greeks, Romans, Celts, and others held it in high regard. The Egyptians considered it an ancient herb, and according to legend, it came from the tears of Isis as she wept for Osiris. In addition to purifying temples and homes with it, the Romans used it medicinally. In medieval times, witches were said to have employed vervain in love potions and in charms to ward off hexes. This plant was also known as simpler's joy. In the past, remedies made with one herb were called simples.

Along with meadowsweet and water mint (*Mentha aquatica*), vervain was one of the three most sacred herbs for ancient Druids. According to Welsh legend, it was an ingredient in Cerridwen's cauldron.

Use long stems of vervain to energetically sweep your ritual and magic space or other areas to remove any form of negativity. Place leaves on your altar to bless the space and empower your rituals. Make an infusion of the leaves to consecrate ritual and divination tools. Place a sachet of dried flowers under your pillow to aid in dream work. This will also encourage dreams of prophecy and help banish nightmares. Grow vervain or scatter dried leaves on your property to attract abundance.

Vervain is associated with the elements air, earth, and fire. Its astrological influence comes from Venus. This plant is associated with the following deities: Cerridwen, Demeter, Diana, Epona, Hermes, Isis, Juno, Jupiter, Mars, Mercury, Persephone, Thor, and Venus.

## In the House

Summer brings outdoor fun as well as sunburn, bug bites and stings, and scrapes and bruises. Saint John's wort can be used to make an all-purpose first aid oil to soothe all of these.

### Soothing Red Oil

¾ cup fresh flowers, leaves, and buds of Saint John's wort
    coarsely chopped

1 pint sweet almond oil

Place the herbs in a clear glass jar and slowly pour in the oil. Gently swirl the contents to mix. Store the jar out of direct light where it will stay at room temperature for two to three weeks. The oil will turn a rich, deep red color. Strain out the plant material and bottle.

In addition to first aid, this also makes a good magical oil for anointing ritual participants and for consecrating candles. Before using it for magical purposes, place the bottle of oil in the light of a full moon.

# July

Shimmering waves of heat rise skyward during the day, and night does not always bring cooling relief. July brings us into high summer, a time to have fun outdoors and enjoy the splendor of the green world. Although there are no sabbats this month, there is magic aplenty with so many plants growing and blooming. Originally called *quintilis*, meaning "the fifth month," the name of this month was changed by Julius Caesar to honor himself.[65]

## On the Calendar
### *July 3: The Dog Days of Summer*
This day traditionally marks the beginning of the dog days of summer, which extend to mid August. These hot days are so named for Sirius, the Dog Star. The name Sirius

---

65    Payack, *A Million Words and Counting*, 176.

comes from Greek and means "scorching" or "searing."[66] In ancient times, this star rose just before the sun during the hottest period of the year.

················

## DOG ROSE
(*Rosa canina*)
> *Also known as beach rose, dagger rose, dog briar, wild briar, and witches' briar

This thicket-forming shrub can reach six to eight feet tall. Its arching stems are studded with hooked thorns that help it climb up anything that is nearby. The pointed, oval leaflets have toothed edges, and are greener than garden roses. The five-petaled flowers are white to pale pink and lightly scented. The plant produces scarlet rosehips in the autumn. Dog rose can be found along sunny roadsides, edges of woodlands and meadows, hedges, and along beaches.

A signal of summer, this simple rose is not the highly fragranced flower extolled by Middle Eastern poets or swooned over by the Victorians. However, what it may lack in fragrance and beauty, it makes up medicinally. Roman physician and botanist Pliny the Elder (23–79 CE) praised its use for many ailments, and it is still widely used in herbal remedies. In the Middle Ages rosehips were carried as a charm against certain diseases. According to folklore, the devil was said to be mortally afraid of roses.

This lovely old-fashioned rose is also a little powerhouse for magic. Enamored with roses in general, fairies are said to enjoy dog rose thickets. Plant one in your garden to invite their blessings. No matter where you find a dog rose, leave an offering underneath it for the fairies.

Hold a leaf or flower between your hands while you ground and center your energy before divination. Also do this before bed to encourage prophetic dreams.

Dog rose is associated with the element water and with fairies.

---

66    Ian Ridpath, *Star Tales* (Cambridge, England: Lutterworth Press, 1988), 40.

*July 8: The Celtic Month of Holly Begins*

Although we associate holly with winter, it comes into flower at this time of year. Flowers produce the bright berries that we love to use for our Yule altars. Now that summer solstice has passed, this tree takes over kingship from oak as the year begins to wane. In the past, it was believed unlucky to take holly indoors except at Yule. In addition, it was considered very unlucky to cut down a living holly tree.

............

## HOLLY

American Holly (*Ilex opaca*)

English Holly (*I. aquifolium*)

   \*Also known as common holly

English holly is a dense, pyramid-shaped tree that reaches thirty to fifty feet tall and half as wide. Its glossy, dark green leaves have wavy margins and sharp spines. American holly reaches twenty-five to fifty feet tall. Its leaves are matte green instead of glossy. Both species produce small white flowers that grow in clusters at the base of the leaf stems. The flowers are inconspicuous and easy to overlook. Holly produces male and female flowers on separate trees, making holly reliant on pollinators such as bees and insects. This means that you need to have one of each tree if you want holly berries, which occur only on the female tree.

With sharp spines, holly leaves are the epitome of protection. To enhance the defense of your home, place three leaves under the front door mat. The leaves can also be used for protection against hostile magic. Tuck a leaf into your purse or wallet to carry for good luck. Dry several clusters of flowers and then sew them into a sachet. Place it under your pillow to enhance dream work, especially divination through dreams. Put fresh holly flowers on your altar for spiritual guidance.

Holly is associated with the elements air, earth, and fire. Its astrological influence comes from Mars and Saturn. This tree is also associated with the following deities: Ares, Cailleach Bheur, Cernunnos, the Dagda, Danu, Freyr, Gaia, Holle, Lugh, and Saturn.

*Figure 20. Holly is associated with the ogham Tinne (left) and the rune Mannaz (right).*

## In the Garden

### Cherries

One of the earliest tree fruits to ripen is the cherry, and everyone has a favorite pie recipe. The tart taste of cherries is great on vanilla ice cream, dipped in chocolate, or straight from the tree. In April we learned what to do with cherry blossoms. Refer to the entry in "April" for more details on cherry trees. Now, let's see what we can do with the fruit.

Just as the flowers are associated with love, so too are the cherries. Squeeze the juice from a cherry and use it to consecrate a red candle for love spells. To attract love, wash two cherry stones (fruit pits), let them dry, and then sew them into a little pouch to carry with you. To help manifest your dreams, take three cherries, and one at a time pull the stems off. As you do this, visualize your wishes. After eating the three cherries, bury the stones as you say:

> *Fruit of abundance, red and round; I commit your seeds to the ground. Manifest the vision I see; blessed cherry, so mote it be.*

### Dill

(*Anethum graveolens* syn. *Peucedanum graveolens*)
*Also known as dill weed, dillseed, dilly, European dill, and garden dill

Reaching three feet tall, dill has an erect, hollow stem. The leaves are ferny, thread-like, and bluish-green. Large, flat umbel clusters of yellow flowers bloom mid to late summer. The tiny oval seeds are flat and ribbed. Dill looks very similar to its cousin fennel. The way to tell them apart is that dill has one stem whereas fennel has multiple stems.

This herb's common name comes from the Norse *dylla*, which means "to soothe" or "to lull," and its species name *graveolens* is Latin, meaning "strong scented."[67] The

---

67   Chevallier, *The Encyclopedia of Medicinal Plants*, 166.

leaves are often referred to as dill weed. Cultivated for thousands of years, dill has been an important culinary and medicinal herb in many cultures.

In addition to being associated with the cult of Dionysus, this plant was used as offerings to Adonis and Bacchus. Later during the Middle Ages, dill was a popular ingredient in love potions and commonly used to provide protection from witches and evil spirits.

With a history of use in love potions, dill also helps to overcome love hexes. Eating dill seeds is helpful for finding balance where lust and desire are concerned. Burn dried leaves and scatter them around your property for defensive magic and to divert black magic from your home. Burning the leaves also purifies a space as does sweeping an area with long dill stalks. Grow dill in your garden to attract luck and wealth. Hang a bundle of dill in your kitchen to invite abundance. Place a couple of flower heads in your workspace to boost creativity and on your altar to support divination.

Dill is associated with the elements air and fire. Its astrological influence comes from Mercury. This herb is also associated with the gods Adonis, Bacchus, and Dionysus.

### Henbane
(*Hyoscyamus niger*)
   *Also known as Belinuntia, black nightshade, devil's eye,
   insane root, and stinking nightshade

Henbane has lance-shaped leaves with wavy edges on stalks that grow up to three feet tall. The brownish-yellow, bell-shaped flowers are marbled with purple veins and have purple centers. The flowers grow at the base of the upper leaves. Although it is often grown as an ornamental plant, henbane has an unpleasant odor and it can be highly toxic if ingested.

Needless to say, don't grow henbane if you have children. However, it makes a nice addition to a witches' garden more for historical reasons than practical use. Although it is used medicinally in some circumstances, it is unsafe for home herbal self-medication.

This plant's common name comes from the Anglo-Saxon *hennbana*, meaning "hen killer" in reference to the belief that poultry would die after eating the seeds.[68] The Celts of Gaul called it *Belinuntia*, meaning "herb of the sun god Bel."[69]

Even though the Greeks used it medicinally, they knew of its lethal properties and, according to legend, used the leaves to crown their dead. Although the Greeks and Romans used it in remedies, henbane's hallucinogenic and poisonous properties effected its reputation in later centuries. By the Middle Ages it became associated with witches and sorcerers who were believed to control the weather and conjure spirits with it.

Because of henbane's association with death, the otherworld, and spirits, you may want to consider drying a stalk of leaves and flowers to place on your altar at Samhain. On November 1, take it outside and burn it in your cauldron.

Henbane is associated with the elements earth and water. Its astrological influence comes from the planet Saturn and the fixed star Ala Corvi. Henbane is associated with the deities Belenus, Hades, Hecate, Jupiter, and the Morrigan.

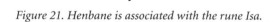

*Figure 21. Henbane is associated with the rune Isa.*

### Hyssop
(*Hyssopus officinalis*)
   *Also known as hedge hyssop

Hyssop has upright, angular stems and reaches about two feet in height. Like other members of the mint family, it has square stems. The lance-shaped leaves are dark green. Tiny purple-blue flowers grow in whorls at the ends of the stems. They bloom from midsummer to early autumn. The stems, leaves, and flowers are aromatic.

---

68  Ivo Pauwels and Gerty Christoffels, *Herbs: Healthy Living with Herbs from Your Own Garden*, trans. Milton Webber (Antwerp, The Netherlands: Struik Publishers, 2006), 138.

69  Ralph Metzner, *The Well of Remembrance: Rediscovering the Earth Wisdom Myths of Northern Europe* (Boston: Shambhala Publications, Inc., 1994), 289.

Hyssop was highly regarded as a medicinal herb by the ancient Greeks and Romans. Because of its strong camphor-like odor, it was also used for cleaning domestic and sacred places. This plant's genus and common names come from the Greek word *hussopos*, which means "holy herb."[70] The Romans used the leaves for culinary purposes including a wine they called *Hyssopites*.[71] By the eighth century it was a mainstay in Anglo-Saxon gardens and remained so throughout Britain well beyond the Middle Ages. Its use for cleaning was carried on for centuries as a strewing herb. Hyssop is still used in home herbal remedies.

Because of its long history of use in cleaning sacred spaces, hyssop is perfect for purifying areas for ritual and consecrating altars. Make a tea with leaves and/or flowers and sprinkle it around the area or on objects to remove negativity. Also add the tea to a pre-ritual bath or for a healing soak. Dip a stem of hyssop in a bowl of fresh water and sprinkle it around your home or property to remove hexes and to provide protection against enchantment. Use several stems like a broom to remove negative energy and to encourage unwanted spirits to move on. Infuse hyssop sprigs in olive oil and use it to anoint participants in ritual. Place a sprig under your bed to aid in fertility, vitality, and any sexual issue. Burning the leaves raises spiritual vibrations.

Hyssop is associated with the elements air and fire. Its astrological influence comes from Jupiter.

### Lavender

English Lavender (*Lavandula angustifolia* syn. *L. officinalis*)
   *Also known as common lavender, elf leaf, and true lavender

Lavender is a bushy evergreen shrub that reaches two or three feet tall and spreads about two feet wide. The lower stems turn dense and woody with age. Small purplish flowers grow in whorls atop leafless stems and bloom from midsummer to early autumn. The slightly fuzzy, needle-like leaves are grayish green or silvery green.

---

70   Claire Kowalchik and William H. Hylton, eds., *Rodale's Illustrated Encyclopedia of Herbs* (Emmaus, PA: Rodale Press, Inc., 1998), 342.

71   Denys J. Charles, *Antioxidant Properties of Spices, Herbs and Other Sources* (New York: Springer Science + Business Media, 2013), 353.

The name lavender was derived from the Latin *lavo*, meaning "to wash," and its species name, *angustifolia*, means "narrow-leaved."[72] As its common name suggests, it has been used for washing since the time of the ancient Greeks and Romans. Throughout Europe during the Middles Ages, lavender was associated with love and was thought to be an aphrodisiac. In addition, it was believed that carrying a sprig of lavender leaves gave a person the ability to see ghosts.

The scent of lavender enhances awareness and intuition for dream work, clairvoyance, and all forms of psychic work. Place fresh or dried flowers and/or leaves wherever you engage in these activities. Lavender's fragrance also fosters concentration for divination and aids in contact with spirit guides. With well-known powers of purification, burn dried leaves and flowers as incense to consecrate sacred space, release negativity, or to provide protection. Carry a dried flower spike in a sachet to attract love or to promote fidelity and renewal in a relationship. A bouquet of lavender flowers on your altar helps to deepen spirituality. Also, save a few bundles of lavender leaves and flowers to toss on a winter fire to scent a room or ritual space.

Lavender is associated with the element air, and its astrological influence comes from Mercury. It is associated with fairies and with the deities Hecate, Vesta, and Saturn.

### Morning Glory and Moonflower

Common Morning Glory (*Ipomoea purpurea* syn.
   *Convolvulus purpureus, Pharbitis purpurea*)

Moonflower (*I. alba* syn. *I. bona-nox, Calonyction aculeatum*)

Morning glory vines can grow six to ten feet long. They have heart-shaped leaves and two-inch-wide flowers that can be blue, pink, red, white, or purplish-blue. These trumpet-shaped flowers have white throats. They open in the morning and close at night or in the rain. There are many species of morning glories. Moonflower vines can grow fifteen feet long. The leaves are rounded with a heart-shaped base. Their five-inch-wide white, fragrant flowers open at dusk. All parts of these plants are poisonous if ingested.

---

72   Coombes, *Dictionary of Plant Names*, 115.

The genus name for these plants come from the Greek *ips*, meaning "worm," and *homoios*, "resembling," in reference to the vines that wind their way up anything nearby.[73] Morning glories and moonflowers previously shared their genus, *Convolvulus*, with their bindweed cousins. According to folk beliefs, witches used morning glories and moonflowers, and the magical power of these plants was stronger when plucked three days before the full moon.

On the night of a new moon, write what you want to bind or secure on a piece of paper, and roll it into a scroll. Use a piece of vine, stripped of its leaves and flowers, and wrap it around the scroll three times as you say:

*Morning glory, moonflower; help me with your sweet power. As I wrap these words of mine; make it so with your vine.*

Hold it between your hands as you send your energy into it and visualize your goal. Take it outside and bury it in the ground.

Use moonflowers to honor lunar goddesses by placing a few on your altar for esbat rituals. If you keep an outdoor altar, place a small trellis behind it for both morning glories and moonflowers to climb so you will have flowers blooming day and night in your sacred space.

Morning glories and moonflowers are associated with the element water. The morning glory's astrological influence comes from Saturn, and moonflower's influence comes from the moon.

### Mugwort
(*Artemisia vulgaris*)
> *Also known as armoise, felon herb, Saint John's plant, and wild wormwood

With reddish-brown stems, this shrubby plant reaches two to six feet tall. Its deeply lobed leaves are dark green on top and silvery underneath. Small, greenish-yellow to reddish-brown flowers grow in clusters and bloom from July to September. It is similar

---

73  Tenenbaum, *Taylor's Encyclopedia of Garden Plants*, 208.

in appearance to motherwort (*Leonurus cardiaca*) and its cousin wormwood (*Artemisia absinthium*). In fact, during the Middle Ages, mugwort was known as motherwort. Mugwort's leaves have a sage-like odor.

Regarded as an herb of great power, mugwort was used for a wide range of medicinal and magical purposes by the Greeks and Romans. Its genus, *Artemisia*, was named after the Greek goddess Artemis. The Egyptians used this plant to honor Isis. Medieval pilgrims used mugwort for a range of medicinal preventatives and for protection against beasts and demons. Circlets and crowns were made with stalks of leaves and worn for protection against evil. In England, mugwort's uses ranged from making beer to keeping moths out of clothes.

Mugwort is instrumental in honing divination skills, especially scrying, as well as for purifying and consecrating divination tools. Make a tea with mugwort leaves, let it cool, and then strain it. Use the tea to cleanse scrying balls and other tools. For items such as tarot decks that you do not want to get wet, make a sachet with dried leaves and wrap it in a cloth with your tools when not in use. Alternatively, burn a few leaves and pass your tools through the smoke.

With strong defensive powers, mugwort protects against dark magic and provides excellent protection for the home. Make a wreath with several stalks of leaves and flowers to hang on your door or over your altar, and visualize it repelling all forms of negativity. To enhance the energy of full or dark moon rituals, place fresh leaves and/or flowers on your altar. Use them to call on the energy of the Goddess.

Mugwort is associated with the elements air, earth, and water. Its astrological influence comes from Venus and the fixed stars Algol, Capella, Deneb Algedi, Polaris, and Regulus. This plant is also associated with the goddesses Artemis, Diana, Hecate, and Isis.

*Figure 22. Mugwort is associated with the rune Raido.*

## Sage

Common Sage (*Salvia officinalis*)

  *Also known as European sage, garden sage, and true sage

Sage grows one to three feet tall and has square, woody base stems covered in down. This plant tends to get bushy and sprawl. Its oblong leaves are light gray-green, veined, and appear wrinkled. Leafy stalks bear whorls of small, blue-purple flowers that bloom early to midsummer. Snip off the flower stalks to extend the leaf harvest.

The genus name, *Salvia*, comes from the Latin *salvare*, which means "to cure" or "make healthy."[74] Considered more for medicinal than culinary purposes, sage has a long history of use by the ancient Egyptians, Greeks, and Romans. It was used throughout Europe, and from the sixteenth century onward it was an important herb to British apothecaries. Drinking sage tea was thought to promote good health and enhance longevity. For those who preferred something stronger, there was sage ale. Common sage is often used for smudging in place of white sage (*Salvia apiana*), which is used as a sacred herb by Native Americans.

Burning a pinch of sage provides focus and stability for clairvoyance, divination, and psychic work. Its grounding energy clears negativity and is instrumental for ritual purification. It is also effective for healing circles. Pass ritual and magical tools through the smoke of burning leaves to cleanse and consecrate them. Also do this to remove negativity and unwanted energy from crystals and gemstones.

Burning sage during meditation is an aid for finding spirit guides. When journeying, wear a sprig of sage leaves for psychic protection and for help in attuning with animal power. Grow sage in your garden or hang a sprig in your home to invite wealth and prosperity. Use a sachet of dried leaves as a charm to help make your wishes come true.

Sage is associated with the elements air and earth. Its astrological influence comes from Jupiter and Mercury, and the fixed star Spica. This plant is also associated with the god Zeus.

---

74  Roberta Wilson, *Aromatherapy: Essential Oils for Vibrant Health and Beauty* (New York: Penguin Putnam, Inc., 2002), 130.

*Figure 23. Sage is associated with the rune Teiwaz.*

## In the Wild
### Datura
(*Datura stramonium*)

    *Also known as devil's apple, devil's trumpet, jimsonweed,
mad apple, and thornapple

Datura is a branching, sprawling plant that grows from two to five feet tall. Its large oval leaves have coarse, unevenly toothed edges. The striking, trumpet-shaped flowers can be white or purplish, and have pointed petals. Covered with spines, the round, walnut-sized seedpod turns brown and splits lengthwise as it ripens. The entire plant has an unpleasant odor. Like its cousins belladonna and henbane, datura is poisonous. In fact, it can be fatal if ingested.

Because of its psychoactive properties, datura has been used in various cultures since ancient times for particular rituals and shamanic practices. Experiences with this plant were said to border on madness. The Egyptians, Greeks, and Romans were familiar with this plant, and in the Middle Ages it was said to have been an ingredient in witches' potions and ointments. Native Americans also used datura.

The spiny seedpod is the source for many of this plant's folk names. The name jimsonweed evolved from Jamestown weed in reference to an incident in 1676 at Jamestown, Virginia.[75] After ingesting the plant in their food, a troop of English soldiers ran amuck in a wild state of delirium. Although datura has several medicinal applications, it is too dangerous for home herbal use.

If you encounter datura in the wild, give a nod to its powers and leave an offering to Hecate, Hades, or other deities of the underworld. Let it serve as a reminder to live and enjoy the light of the living.

---

75   Dobelis, *Magic and Medicine of Plants*, 226.

Datura is associated with the element water, the goddess Hecate, and the god Hades. Its astrological influence comes from Saturn.

### Elecampane
(*Inula helenium*)
    \*Also known as elf dock, elfwort, and inula

With long, lance-shaped leaves, elecampane's erect stem grows three to six feet tall. Its bright flowers have tangled rays of petals, making them look like scraggly, yellow daisies or overgrown dandelions. They bloom from July to September. Elecampane can be found along roadsides, fields, clearings, and in waste areas.

While there are a number of theories about the Greek word *inula* in its genus name, sources agree that the Romans added *campana* to the name in reference to an area near Naples where it grew. *Inula campana* evolved into elecampane in English. The species name *helenium* is in reference to Helen of Troy. According to differing legends, she was either holding a sprig of this plant or elecampane flowers grew where her tears fell when Paris abducted her.

The Greeks and Romans used elecampane medicinally. In addition to its healing properties, the roots were used to make candied sweets during the Middle Ages. Elecampane has also been used as a flavoring for liqueurs, particularly absinthe and vermouth.

Sprinkle any part of the dried herb to create a protective circle before ritual or magic work, especially when doing love spells. Dried leaves burned with incense before divination enhances psychic abilities. Place sprigs of flowers on your altar to aid in contacting nature spirits.

Elecampane is associated with the element air. Its astrological influence comes from Mercury.

*Figure 24. Elecampane is associated with the ogham Ebad.*

## In the House
### *A Rose by Any Other Name*
Rose (*Rosa* spp.)

The fragrance of roses is a scent that is recognized worldwide and has been written about throughout history. Linked with romance and allure, roses were also symbols of spirituality and mysticism. Not only do roses smell wonderful, but they also have healing properties, and the petals are edible. Of course the fruit, rosehips, are edible too. Resist pruning faded flowers to let the rosehips form.

There are thousands of books on the subject and a dizzying number of rose varieties and cultivars. The roses that we grow in our gardens are usually classified into three main groups: species roses, old garden or old-fashioned roses, and modern roses. The species roses are the ones that have grown wild for hundreds or thousands of years. They have a single flower with five petals. The dog rose, covered earlier in this chapter, is a species rose.

The old garden or old-fashioned roses (sometimes called heritage or historic roses) are hybrids that were introduced before 1867.[76] Their flowers have dense ruffled layers of petals. While they bloom once in a season, they tend to be more fragrant than their modern cousins. Modern roses were introduced after 1867. These bloom more than once in a season, have a larger flower size, and have a longer vase life.

Many roses are at their height of blooming this month, making it a good time to add them to our magical repertoire. In addition to the actual flower, we can use rosewater and rose oil. Both are easy to make. The best time to pick flowers is when they are just coming into full bloom. Cut them from the plant in the morning after the dew has dried and before the heat of the day sets in. Gently pull the petals apart.

One way to make rosewater is to firmly pack rose petals into a mason jar and then pour in enough distilled water to cover them. Put the lid on and set the jar in a sunny place. Let the petals soak for about twenty-four hours and then strain out the petals.

Another way to make rosewater is to place the rose petals in a pan, cover with distilled water, and put the lid on the pan. Warm the petals on low heat on the stove for a few minutes. Remove from the heat, and let the petals infuse for three to four hours, and then strain.

---

76 Tenenbaum, *Taylor's Encyclopedia of Garden Plants*, 342.

To make rose oil, use a lightweight oil such as sweet almond. Place the petals in a mason jar and pour in enough oil to cover them. Store in a dark cupboard at room temperature for three to four weeks, and then strain.

Sprinkle rosewater around your home to attract peace and aid in dealing with family issues. In addition, the healing energy of roses brings happiness, friendship, and luck to the home. Rose oil is good for consecrating amulets and charms. Use candles prepared with rose oil in banishing and binding spells and for releasing hexes. Sprinkle rosewater around your altar when engaging in clairvoyance, communicating with spirits, and psychic work in general. To aid in divination or encourage prophetic dreams, rub rose oil on your wrists where your body heat will aid in releasing a rose scent for several hours. Alternatively, add a few rose petals to a cup of herbal tea and drink it before a divination session or before bed.

Rose is associated with the element water, and its astrological influence comes from Venus. This flower is associated with fairies and the following deities: Adonis, Aphrodite, Cupid, Demeter, Eros, Flora, Freya, Hathor, Holle, Isis, and Venus.

# August

In August, the hot, humid weather gives plants time to complete their annual cycle of growth. Dazzling thunderstorms punctuate lazy days as summer slowly winds down, yet autumn seems a distant horizon. Like June, this month was originally named by number and called *sextilis* because it was the sixth month on the Roman calendar.[77] Caesar Augustus changed the name of this month to honor himself.

## On the Calendar
### August 1: Lammas/Lughnasadh
Although the shortening length of the day is just starting to become noticeable, daylight hours still seem long as we slowly drift toward autumn. Lammas marks the first harvest. The name Lammas comes from the Anglo-Saxon *hlafmas*, meaning "loaf-mass," a

---

77    Payack, *A Million Words and Counting*, 176.

celebration when the first loaves of bread were made from fresh-cut grain.[78] At this sabbat the god was often portrayed as the Corn King, who was symbolically sacrificed and his seed laid to rest in the womb of the Mother Goddess.

The word "corn" in this regard is a reference to cereal grains in general, not the maize of North America. In fact, barley was the traditional grain that was later superseded by wheat. Place fresh-cut herbs and fresh-baked bread on your altar for this sabbat. Give thought to where your food comes from and the cycles that helped create and nurture the plants.

Despite the Gaelic name Lughnasadh being a reference to the god Lugh, who is associated with the sun, this is not a solar celebration. It is one of the cross-quarter days associated with the earth. In Ireland, this date originally marked the funeral feast of Tailltiu, Lugh's foster mother, who was considered an earth mother.

### August 5: The Celtic Month of Hazel Begins

Young catkin-bearing hazel branches were commonly called wands, and according to legend, Mercury's winged wand was made of hazel. When hazel is found growing with apple and hawthorn, it is said that these mark the boundary of a magical place.

............
### HAZEL

Common Hazel (*Corylus avellana*)
  *Also known as common filbert and English hazel

American Hazelnut (*C. americana*)
  *Also known as American filbert

Both of these hazels are shrubby, multi-trunked trees. The common hazel reaches fifteen to twenty feet tall and produces prominent yellow catkins in late winter. The American hazelnut grows to about fifteen feet tall and twelve feet wide. It produces yellow-brown male catkins up to three inches long. Both trees have pointed leaves that are heavily veined and toothed.

---

78  Ferguson, *The Magickal Year*, 158.

The genus name for hazelnut comes from the Greek *korys*, meaning "hood," which refers to the shape of the husk that covers the nut. Likewise the name hazel, from the Anglo Saxon *haesel*, meaning "bonnet," also refers to the husk.[79] Small, round nuts are called cobs or hazelnuts, and the larger ones are called filberts. That said, the names hazelnut and filbert are often used interchangeably.

Hazelnuts were associated with the mystic rites of both Mercury and Apollo. Hazel branches used for divining rods were said to be particularly potent if cut on Midsummer's Eve. In Celtic mythology, hazelnuts were closely associated with salmon and water. Although the details of legends differ, the hazelnut was considered a repository of wisdom. This wisdom was passed along to the salmon that ate the nuts as well as anyone who ate the salmon.

Place a circle of hazel leaves on your altar to aid you in all forms of magic. During divination sessions, place a forked hazel branch on your altar or table for guidance. Hang a hazel stick above your altar or over a doorway to provide protection and defense. Use a hazel stick to draw a magic circle for extra protection. In place of a stick, use a brown candle into which you have carved the ogham character associated with hazel. Place a handful of dried leaves in your workspace to stimulate inspiration for creative projects. The leaves are also an aid when initiating changes, plus they provide support for all forms of communication. Leaves or a small twig on your altar during meditation will help you connect with inner wisdom.

Hazel is associated with the elements air, fire, and water. Its astrological influence comes from Mercury and the sun. This tree is associated with the following deities: Aphrodite, Apollo, Arianrhod, Artemis, Boann, Danu, Diana, Manannan, Mercury, Ogma, Thor, and Venus.

*Figure 25. Hazel is associated with the ogham Coll.*

---

79   Frederic Rosengarten, Jr., *The Book of Edible Nuts* (Mineola, NY: Dover Publications, 2004), 95.

# In the Garden

## *Aconite*

Common Monkshood (*Aconitum napellus*)

    *Also known as blue rocket, friar's cap, and wolfsbane

Wolfsbane (*A. lycoctonum*)

    *Also known as monkshood and northern wolfsbane

The aconites are best known for their distinctive, elongated flowers. These plants form clumps that can be two feet tall and wide from which graceful spires arise with dense clusters of flowers. The leaves of wolfsbane are light green with deeply cut lobes. The flower spires can be two to six feet tall. Wolfsbane flowers are yellow or whitish yellow, and sometimes purple. Common monkshood has dark green leaves with deeply cut lobes. Its spires can reach three to four feet tall with dark blue-violet flowers.

These cousins cause a lot of confusion because they look so similar and their names have been used interchangeably. In ancient times, both of these plants were called wolfsbane. According to legend they were used to poison bait and arrows for hunting wolves and other wild animals that threatened villages. In the Middle Ages the plants became known as monkshood because the flower shape was thought to look like the cowls worn by monks.

All parts of wolfsbane are highly poisonous. Although common monkshood is used in Chinese and Ayurvedic medicine, without proper preparation of plant material it is toxic and not used in Western herbal remedies. That said, monkshood has been grown as an ornamental garden plant for centuries.

According to mythology, the aconites sprang from the foaming mouths of Cerberus, the triple-headed dog of Greek and Roman mythology that guarded the entrance to the underworld. In other legends, Hecate used these plants to create poison arrows called elf bolts. Aristotle is said to have used one of the aconites to commit suicide.

Grow either of these plants on your property for protection, especially against shapeshifters. Growing them also honors Hecate. Be sure to plant aconites only where children do not have access to them. In addition, these plants should be handled only while wearing gloves. Because of their association with death, place an offering under one of these plants when a loved one passes to the otherworld and ask that the plant's devas provide guidance for them. Also associated with enchantment, place an offering under the plant on a full moon to foster magical energy.

The aconites are associated with the element water and the goddess Hecate. Their astrological influence comes from Saturn.

*Figure 26. The Aconites are associated with the rune Perth.*

## *Basil*
(*Ocimum basilicum*)
   *Also known as common basil, French basil, and sweet basil

Basil is a bushy plant that reaches one to two feet tall. Its oval leaves have prominent veins and distinctive downward curling edges. They are yellow-green to dark green and very fragrant. White, pink, or purple flowers grow at the tops of the stems and bloom from midsummer to autumn. With a strong, spicy aroma, it is probably no surprise that basil is one of the most popular herbs in modern gardens.

Basil's genus and species names come from Greek meaning "aromatic" or "smell," and "kingly" or "royal," respectively.[80] In later centuries the French called it *herbe royale*. Basil is thought to have come from the plant known as holy basil (*Ocimum sanctum*), which originated in India, and according to legend, was transported to Greece by Alexander the Great.

The ancient Egyptians, Greeks, and Romans used this herb for medicinal and culinary purposes. During the Middle Ages basil was used as a strewing herb, scattered on floors to freshen and clear the air as well as to protect homes against witches. In Italy, a potted basil plant was traditionally given as a love token. It was also a signal when placed on a woman's windowsill or balcony that she was ready to receive the affection of her suitor.

---

80   Rosemary Gladstar, *Medicinal Herbs: A Beginner's Guide* (North Adams, MA: Storey Publishing, 2012), 53.

Inhaling the scent of fresh basil leaves bolsters divination skills and is instrumental in developing psychic abilities, especially clairvoyance. Stimulating and refreshing, basil also brings mental clarity for decision-making. Use fresh or dried leaves to attract love as well as to release hexes and banish negativity. Bring a potted basil plant into the home to promote healthy relationships and smooth out problems between lovers especially where fidelity is concerned. Make a tea with the leaves and then sprinkle a little of it in each room to restore harmony to the household. Give a potted basil plant as a house-warming gift to bring luck and prosperity to the receiver.

Basil is associated with the element fire. Its astrological influence comes from Mars, Pluto, and Venus.

### Borage
(*Borago officinalis*)
 *Also known as bee bread, bugloss, burrage, and star flower

The hallmark of borage is its intensely blue, star-shaped flowers that grow in drooping clusters. Its gray-green, oval leaves are pointed and have prominent veins. The hollow, upright stems have many leafy branches. Both the stems and leaves are covered with tiny hairs. Borage grows one to three feet tall. Sprawling and drooping branches give the plant a rounded shape.

In addition to a range of medicinal purposes, the Greeks used borage to flavor wine. Roman naturalist and philosopher Pliny the Elder called the plant *Euphrosinum* because it was said to bring happiness.[81] This plant was used for courage and strength by both Roman and Celtic warriors. The name borage comes from the Celtic word *borrach*, meaning "a person of courage."[82] In Wales it was called *llawenlys*, "herb of gladness."[83] Whether or not it provides courage, medicinally borage helps deal with stress.

---

81   Ann Bonar, *Herbs: A Complete Guide to the Cultivation and Use of Wild and Domesticated Herbs* (New York: MacMillan Publishing Co., 1985), 50.

82   Carr-Gomm and Carr-Gomm, *The Druid Plant Oracle*, 20.

83   Julia Jones and Barbara Deer, *The Country Diary of Garden Lore* (London: Dorling Kindersley Ltd., 1987), 50.

Borage flowers are edible and make a nice addition to summer drinks and salads. Eat a few to energetically aid in expanding awareness for clairvoyance and general psychic work. During divination sessions, place fresh flowers on your table or altar to enhance abilities. Call on the power of borage to help initiate changes in your life by floating several flowers in a bowl of water on your altar while you visualize what you want to manifest. Afterward, let the flowers dry, burn them in your cauldron, and then scatter the ashes outdoors as you repeat the visualization.

Borage is associated with the elements air and fire. It astrological influence comes from Jupiter.

### Catnip
(*Nepeta cataria*)
    *Also known as catmint, catnep, cat's play, and field balm

Reaching up to three feet tall, catnip has heart-shaped, grayish-green leaves that are covered in downy hairs. Growing in dense whorls at the end of the main stem and branches, its white or pale lavender flowers are marked with purple spots. The flowers bloom from July through October.

Since the time of the Romans, catnip was a popular garden herb for culinary and medicinal purposes. According to legend, chewing the root provided courage and was used by executioners before carrying out their duties. In England it was often used for tea before trade with the East brought in black tea. Today it is used medicinally as an herbal tea to calm the nerves. Contrary to some rumors, smoking it does not provide a high.

The oil that the plant releases to ward off insects attracts cats. More of this oil is released whenever the plant it bruised, which inadvertently happens when it is transplanted. If you want to grow it in your garden without attracting all the cats in the neighborhood, sow seeds instead of buying plants and leave it where it grows.

To enhance animal magic or to attract benevolent spirits, sprinkle dried leaves on your altar. Quite naturally, catnip aids in bonding psychically with a cat. Drinking a cup of catnip tea is effective for increasing abilities in dream and psychic work. To make the tea, pour one cup of boiling water over two tablespoons of dried leaves, and let it steep, covered, for ten minutes. Catnip should not be ingested during pregnancy. Also, if you don't grow your own, make sure to purchase food-grade catnip if you plan to use it for tea.

Catnip is associated with the elements air and water. Its astrological influence comes from Venus and the fixed star Deneb Algedi. This plant is also associated with the goddesses Bast and Sekhmet.

## Chamomile

Roman Chamomile (*Chamaemelum nobile* syn. *Anthemis nobilis*)
 *Also known as common chamomile, English chamomile, garden chamomile, and sweet chamomile

German Chamomile (*Matricaria recutita* syn. *M. chamomilla*)
 *Also known as blue chamomile, Hungarian chamomile, mayweed, and wild chamomile

With branching stems, German chamomile stands erect and can reach two or three feet in height. Although it is an annual, it readily self-seeds, giving the impression of being a biennial or perennial. Roman chamomile is a perennial, spreading herb with stems that creep along the ground. It is usually less than nine inches high. Both chamomiles have small, daisy-like flowers with white petals and yellow centers that grow at the ends of the stems. German chamomile flowers are less fragrant than the apple-scented Roman. Both plants have feathery leaves; however, the leaves of Roman chamomile are a little coarser.

Used interchangeably, both types of chamomile have been popular in European herbal medicine since antiquity. Roman chamomile was used as a strewing herb because stepping on the flowers releases their sweet fragrance.

Well known for physical and emotional healing, chamomile brings clarity and success in communication. Brew a cup of tea with two teaspoons of crumbled dried flowers and one cup of boiling water. Let it steep for at least ten minutes, and then strain. Drink a cup before going to bed to enhance dream work, or drink a cup before divination sessions. The tea also aids in grounding energy for psychic work, especially Roman chamomile when channeling. Use the tea to purify and consecrate altars and ritual or magic tools. With two stems of German chamomile, make the letter X on your altar to counteract hexes. Use the flowers in spells to attract love, luck, money, and prosperity.

Chamomile is associated with the elements air and water. Its astrological influence comes from the sun. Chamomile is also associated with the gods Balder and Cernunnos.

## *Sunflower*

Common Sunflower (*Helianthus annuus*)
    *Also known as annual sunflower

There are about eighty species of sunflowers; however, this is the quintessential one that can grow over ten feet tall. It has thick branching stems and coarse, heart-shaped leaves covered with rough hairs. Its large, yellow-rayed flower head tracks the sun's daily journey across the sky. The flower head can measure four to twelve inches wide.

Its genus name comes from the Greek *helios*, meaning "sun," and *anthos*, "flower."[84] Indigenous to the North American prairies, all parts of the plant were used by Native Americans for a wide range of medicinal remedies. Additionally, it was considered a ceremonial medicine plant, especially for war dances.

Growing sunflowers in the garden brings prosperity to your home. If you don't grow them in your garden, purchase a few flowers and sprinkle the petals around your property as you say:

*Sunflower, sunflower, bright and yellow; help us feel calm and mellow. Beautiful flower, bright as gold; bring prosperity to this household.*

Sunflower petals add strength to spells for attracting money. A sachet of petals under the pillow brings clarity for solving problems and to dream work. Burn a small piece of dried leaf as you visualize what you want to release from your life. This can also be done to dispel negative energy. To help manifest desires, make a wish as you float petals in your bath water.

Sunflower is associated with the element fire, and its astrological influence comes from the sun. This flower is associated with the goddesses Demeter and Modron and the gods Apollo and Helios.

---

84   Tenenbaum, *Taylor's Encyclopedia of Garden Plants*, 188.

## In the Wild

### Agrimony

Common Agrimony (*Agrimonia eupatoria*)

   \*Also known as cockleburr, liverwort, philanthropos, sticklewort,
    and stickwort

Agrimony leaves are comprised of lance-shaped leaflets that are deeply veined and coarsely toothed. Stems growing two to four feet tall hold dense clusters of yellow flowers. The whole plant is slightly aromatic and the flowers have a richly scented, slightly spicy odor. The five-petaled flowers bloom from June through August. Seed capsules form burrs that get stuck on clothing or animals as they pass by. Agrimony is usually found at the edge of woods, fields, and wastelands.

The genus name *Agrimonia* comes from the Greek *argemone*, which was a name given to plants used for healing the eyes.[85] The species name *eupatoria* was derived from the name of a Persian king, Mithradates Eupator (120–63 BCE), who was a skilled herbalist. Throughout the ancient world, agrimony was used for a range of ailments, and it is still used in herbal medicine today.

According to legends, witches used this plant to cast spells as well as to break them. Also, hanging a sachet of agrimony in the home was said to protect against evil spirits. This plant is also associated with deep sleep.

To send a hex back to the hexer, burn a handful of dried leaves in your cauldron as you say:

*Agrimony, agrimony, herb of strength and power, return this spell to the hexer within the hour.*

Say this incantation three times, and when the ashes are cool, take them outside and bury them in the ground.

To dispel any negativity and bless a new home before moving in, burn a pinch of dried leaves as you walk through the house. Whenever you want to banish bad energy

---

85   David W. Sifton, ed., *The PDR Family Guide to Natural Medicines and Healing Therapies* (New York: Ballantine Books, 1999), 259.

from your home, add a quart of boiling water to two handfuls of leaves and/or flowers and let it steep for a half an hour. Strain it and use the infusion when washing floors or other cleaning throughout the home.

Burn a dried leaf and smudge yourself with the smoke to cleanse your aura. In addition, add an infusion of agrimony to your bath water to create a personal protective barrier against negativity. When you are out walking and find burrs, take a few home with you and place them on your altar to bring protection to your home and during magic or ritual.

Agrimony is associated with the element air. Its astrological influence comes from Jupiter and Mercury.

### Arnica
(*Arnica montana*)
   *Also known as leopard's bane, mountain daisy, and wolf's bane

With round, hairy stems, arnica grows from one to three feet tall. The bright green upper leaves are toothed and slightly hairy; the lower leaves have rounded ends. The daisy-like flowers are bright yellow-orange and are two to three inches wide. They bloom in July and August. This plant is found in pastures and woodlands.

Although arnica was widely used in German folk medicine during the Middle Ages, it is seldom used today. When it is, it is used externally. Also, arnica should not be applied to broken skin, as it can be toxic.

Like the plant more commonly known as wolfsbane (*Aconitum lycoctonum*), arnica was used to poison bait for wild animals. However, the reason for the reference to leopards in one of its folk names is unknown. The genus name *Arnica* was derived from the Greek *arnakis*, which means "lamb's skin."[86] This is a reference to the leaves, which sometimes have a wooly texture. The species name *montana*, means "of mountains."[87]

---

86   Rosemary Gladstar and Pamela Hirsch, eds., *Planting the Future: Saving Our Medicinal Herbs* (Rochester, VT: Healing Arts Press, 2000), 60.

87   Coombes, *Dictionary of Plant Names*, 30.

Use dried leaves and/or flowers for protection. Crumble and sprinkle them at the corners of your house as you visualize the energy of this plant rising and creating a dome of safety. As you do this, say three times:

*Arnica, leopard's bane, powerful plant; I call on you, my wish to grant. With your energy make a dome; to protect this house and loving home.*

Raising energy in your home with arnica helps quell restless spirits, too. Also, place a sprig of leaves on your altar to increase and enhance your psychic abilities during divination.

### Honeysuckle
Common Honeysuckle (*Lonicera periclymenum*)
   *Also known as European honeysuckle, love bind,
      wild honeysuckle, and woodbine
Italian Honeysuckle (*L. caprifolium*)
   *Also known as goat leaf and Italian woodbine

There are about two hundred species of honeysuckle; some are shrubs and others are vines. The two included here are twining climbing vines with woody stems that can grow ten to twenty feet in length. They both have rounded leaves and whorls of thin, tubular flowers at the end of the stems. The common honeysuckle has pale to medium yellow flowers and dull gray to bluish-green leaves. It produces dark red berries in the autumn. Italian honeysuckle has pale yellow to pinkish or purplish-tinged flowers and produces orange-red berries in the autumn. Its leaves are dark green above and bluish-green underneath.

The species name for Italian honeysuckle comes from Greek and means "goat's leaf."[88] It was so named because goats enjoy eating the leaves. Common honeysuckle's species name comes from the Greek hero Periclymenus, who was one of the Argonauts as well as a shape shifter. The common name honeysuckle comes from the practice of tearing off the bottom of the flower to suck out the honey-sweet nectar. According to folklore, honeysuckle flowers were not taken indoors where there were young girls because it was believed the scent would give them erotic dreams.

---

88   *Ibid.*, 121.

Honeysuckle vines wind in a sun-wise direction and grow tightly around trees or anything in their paths. A honeysuckle stick was believed to guarantee good luck especially in love. This stick is a hazel branch around which a honeysuckle vine has grown. When the vine is removed, the stick has a twisted appearance. According to folklore, if a man carried one as a walking stick, he would be able to call on the woman of his dreams. Because of honeysuckle's tight embrace, it was sometimes called love bind.

Place fresh honeysuckle flowers on your bedside table to aid in dream work. Also do this to encourage dreams of love and passion. Before going to sleep, spend a few minutes holding the flowers to your nose to enjoy their fragrance. Dried flowers and leaves in a sachet hung over the bed fosters fidelity and affection between partners. Place a handful of flowers and/or leaves on your altar to aid in magic work or to increase psychic powers. A honeysuckle vine growing near the house brings luck.

Honeysuckle is associated with the element earth. Its astrological influence comes from Jupiter, Mars, and Mercury.

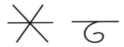

*Figure 27. Honeysuckle is associated with the oghams Ebad (left) and Uilleann (right).*

## In the House
### *Harvesting and Drying Plants*

Harvest leaves and flowers after the morning dew has evaporated. Chant as you harvest and prepare them for drying to set your intention for their magical use. Herbs grown for their leaves are usually harvested throughout the season and before the plants flower. This is when leaves are at their height of potency for taste, medicinal purposes, and magical power. Flowers are at their peak when they first open or just before they fully open.

Flowers can be harvested by pinching them off by hand or by cutting them with scissors. Handle them gently to avoid bruising. Use scissors to harvest stems and leaves. Leaves should be cut off rather than pulled as this may damage the plant. Brush or shake off any dirt or bugs. If you are going to hang plants for drying, cut the entire stem, and then remove the flowers and/or leaves after the plant dries

Air-drying herbs, by hanging them in bunches or laying them on screens, is a simple and traditional way to preserve plants. This method works best in a darkened location with low humidity, good airflow, and a steady, warm temperature. You may find the right conditions in a corner of a room, a porch, shed, attic, or even a large closet where linens or clothes can be scented as the herbs dry.

Gather herbs early in the day and do not rinse them unless they are muddy. If you do rinse them, lay them out on paper towels and let them dry before gathering into bunches. It is important to bundle the same type of plant together, rather than mixing them. Different types of plants dry at different rates because the moisture content varies.

Bundle up to ten stems together with rubber bands, twist ties, or yarn. Attach several bunches upside down to a wire coat hanger with enough space between them so air can circulate freely. A wooden laundry rack can be set up wherever the conditions are right and can hold a number of herb-ladened coat hangers. Make sure the bunches are not touching each other and that they are not right up against a wall or other structure.

For screen drying herbs, a clean window screen works well. As an alternative, a piece of cheesecloth, muslin, or brown paper with small holes poked through it can be attached to an old picture frame to make a drying screen. Lay out the herbs in a single layer. The screens can be set on laundry racks, which will enable good air circulation.

Check your screens and bundles every day. Plants will feel slightly brittle when they are completely dry. Leaves and flowers should be stripped from the stems for storage. Keep them in airtight containers away from direct light.

Seeds should be left to ripen on the plant before they are harvested. Seeds usually start out green and then turn a different color when ripe. Check them every day because the seeds will drop to the ground. You will need a cloth or paper bag to harvest them. When they appear to be ripe, gently bend the stalk until the seed head is over a cloth placed on the ground or inside a bag. Shake the plant so the seeds fall. Alternatively, once the seed head is in a bag, cut the stalk off the plant, hang it somewhere dry, and just let the seeds fall off. If you are using a cloth, draw it up over the seed head and secure it to the stem before cutting it. Store the seeds in airtight containers away from direct light.

# September

As summer draws to an end, nights turn chilly, yet many afternoons are warm and fair as we begin that slow slide into autumn. This turning of the wheel of the year brings dramatic changes with foliage blazing into brilliant colors and summer birds gathering in huge flocks for their journey south. This is a time for gathering in and drawing abundance into our lives. This month takes its name from the Latin *septem*, meaning "seven" as it was the seventh month on the Roman calendar.[89]

## On the Calendar
### *September 2: The Celtic Month of Vine/Bramble Begins*
While vine has come to include the grapevine, it actually refers to the blackberry vines that populated the hedgerows in the British Isles and formed thorny thickets. The

---

89   Payack, *A Million Words and Counting*, 176.

name of the ogham character Muin comes from a Gaelic word meaning "thicket."[90] Wine has been produced from blackberries for many centuries.

......................

## BLACKBERRY

American Blackberry (*Rubus villosus*)

European Blackberry (*R. fruticosus*)
 *Also known as wild blackberry

Both are also known as bramble, brambleberry, cloudberry,
 and dewberry

Blackberry bushes are sprawling shrubs with woody, arching stems called canes. Canes tend to take root where their tips rest on the ground. Blackberry leaves are comprised of three to five coarsely serrated leaflets. They are oval and dark green on top and pale underneath. White, five-petaled flowers grow in clusters at the ends of the stems. Each flower produces a berry, which is actually a cluster of little fruits. The berries change from green to red to black as they ripen. They are fully ripe when dull black, not glossy. The European blackberry was instrumental in the development of modern garden cultivars.

In European folk medicine, the arching canes were believed to have magical properties, and people crept underneath the arches or passed children through gaps in the bush for particular cures. Blackberry bushes were also believed to protect against evil. In parts of England, they were sometimes planted or placed on graves with the belief that they would keep the dead in place. There was a widespread belief that blackberries should not be eaten after a certain date, which varied by region. This ban usually had to do with the devil or witches. Also, warm weather at the end of September was known as a blackberry summer.

Grow a blackberry bush on your property to attract fairies, or set out a small bowl of berries as a token of friendship with them. Eat a handful of blackberries before magic work or when working with the fairy realm. Burn dried leaves in spells to attract money, or sprinkle them around your property to draw luck. Make a wreath with several prickly canes to hang above your altar or on your front door for protective energy. Place a

---

90 Niall MacCoitir, *Irish Trees: Myths, Legends & Folklore* (Cork, Ireland: The Collins Press, 2003), 167.

blackberry cane alongside your altar to aid in grounding energy after rituals. Also, because blackberries are associated with Brigid, gather enough to make jam or wine and use it to honor her at Imbolc.

Blackberry is associated with the element water, and its astrological influence comes from the moon and Venus. This plant is associated with fairies and the deities Brigid, the Dagda, Danu, Freya, and Manannan.

*Figure 28. Blackberry is associated with the ogham Muin.*

### September 14: Nutting Day

In England, it was customary to go to the woods on this date to gather nuts. By contrast, September 21st was called Devil's Nutting Day, and people were warned to stay out of the woods because the devil would be gathering nuts on that day.

#### HAZELNUT

Hazelnuts can be gathered from late August to early September; however, they were regarded as particularly magical when gathered on this date. The hazelnut husk will still be green even when the nut is ripe. The nut itself is light brown. After picking, store them in a dry place until the husk turns brown and it will be easier to remove. To eat them, you will also have to crack the inner shell.

Use hazelnuts in spells for initiating change. Place them on your desk or workspace to enhance creativity. Eat a few hazelnuts before any form of magic or divination, especially clairvoyance.

Hazelnuts can also be eaten before shamanic journeying to aid in acquiring knowledge. Keep some for divination at Samhain. For more about the hazel tree, refer to the entry in "August."

## Beechnut

American Beech (*Fagus grandifolia*)
   \*Also known as white beech

Common Beech (*F. sylvatica*)
   \*Also known as European beech

Often described as stately, the beech tree has a wide spreading canopy. The American beech averages fifty to seventy feet tall with smooth, gray bark. The pointed, oval leaves are about five inches long and have saw-tooth edges. They are dull green on top and lighter underneath. Flowers are clustered together in little yellow or reddish, spiky balls in the early spring and later develop into beechnuts. The common beech is slightly smaller, reaching about fifty or sixty feet tall. Its bark is a darker gray, its leaves are shorter with wavy edges, and its flowers are yellowish-green. The leaves of both trees turn yellow-bronze in the autumn.

The beechnuts are encased in spiny, woody husks. These can be hard to open but give them a few days indoors and they open on their own splitting into four sections. They look like spiny, four-petaled flowers when they open. The edible three-sided nut forms an irregular triangle. Like the hazelnut, beechnuts were believed to impart wisdom. They were also used as amulets.

Use beechnuts in spells to manifest what you seek. Place a few husks on a shelf in the kitchen to attract abundance and prosperity to your home. Eat a few of the nuts to foster creativity and encourage second sight. Save some for Samhain to enhance contact with ancestors.

Beech is associated with the elements fire and water. Its astrological influence comes from Saturn. This tree is also associated with the following deities: Apollo, Bacchus, Cerridwen, Diana, Dionysus, Freya, Frigg, Holle, Loki, Odin, and Zeus.

*Figure 29. Beechnut is associated with the ogham Emancoll and the runes Nauthiz and Perth (shown left to right).*

............
### ACORN

Of course, we can't forget acorns. Through the centuries, people have marveled at how a small seed can produce such an amazingly large tree. For more information about the oak, refer to the entry in "June."

Use an acorn in spells to manifest what you need. Carry one for protection or place several on a windowsill to protect your home. An acorn on your altar during ritual or meditation aids in connecting with ancient wisdom. Place three acorn cups (the top of the nut) in a row on a kitchen windowsill and ask for abundance, blessings, and love for your home and family. Leave several acorn cups in your garden with gifts for fairies.

### September 22/23: Mabon/Autumn Equinox

Mabon is a celebration of the beauty and bounty of the earth and a time to pause and give thanks. In the past, the autumn harvest was a series of celebrations that took place in the fields as each crop was successfully taken in. The most well-known component of these celebrations was creating a corn dolly from the last sheaf of grain.

As previously mentioned, corn in this regard refers to grain crops in general and not maize. Most often the traditional corn dolly was not in human form. Instead, stalks with seed heads attached were braided and twisted into various shapes, decorated with flowers, and tied with ribbons. The corn dolly symbolically held the spirit of the grain and was usually kept in the home until spring when it was put into the first-plowed furrow along with seeds. The corn dolly also represented the cycle from life to death and eventual new life.

To make a simple corn dolly, you will need three pieces of straw with the seed heads attached. Soak the stalks in water overnight so they will be pliable and can be bent without breaking. Tie them together with a piece of thick thread an inch or so below the seed heads. Braid the stalks together but leave about a third of the stalks unbraided at the bottom. Tie another piece of thread around the stalks to keep the braid in place. Bring both ends of the braided section together to create a loop and secure it with another piece of thread. Lay it flat and spread out the ends, alternating the seed heads between the stalk ends. Place a light weight on it to keep it flat as it dries. Add a ribbon along with a few dried flowers or sprigs of herbs to finish it.

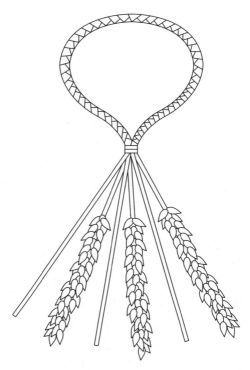

*Figure 30. A simple corn dolly can be made with three stalks of straw.*

Like Lammas, loaves of bread made with newly cut grain were important at Mabon. Place nuts, fruit, leaves, straw stalks, ivy, and fresh-baked bread on your altar as you celebrate the harvest and give thanks.

### September 30: The Celtic Month of Ivy Begins

Ivy is associated with the Goddess because it grows in a spiral, which is one of her symbols. Use ivy on your altar to symbolize your spiritual journey through the wheel of the year: in winter we follow the spiral of energy down and within, and in the spring we follow it back up into the light for our own symbolic rebirth.

.......

## Ivy
Common Ivy (*Hedera helix*)
  *Also known as English ivy

Ivy is a familiar evergreen vine with woody stems. Its dark green leaves have three to five shallow lobes. There are hundreds of cultivars based on leaf shape, size, and variegation. Ivy grows as a climbing vine or trailing ground cover. It has two stages: In the juvenile stage, it climbs and spreads. In the adult stage, it becomes more like a shrub and produces clusters of greenish-white flowers that develop into blue-black berries.

Just as circlets of laurel were used as crowns for athletes in ancient Greece, ivy was used to crown poets. Ivy was associated with Dionysus because it was regarded as an antidote to drunkenness. Binding the brow with ivy was supposed to prevent intoxication while also enhancing the effects of alcohol. In England, ivy-covered poles called ale bushes were the forerunner of pub signs.

According to folklore, if ivy grew on the walls of a house, the occupants were safe from witches. If the ivy died, the family was in for disaster. According to love divination, if a young woman put an ivy leaf in her pocket, the first man she encountered after leaving the house would become her husband. The early Christian church in England forbid the use of ivy decorations in churches because of its association with Paganism.

Grow ivy on your property or place it as a houseplant in a front window to guard against negative energy and to attract good luck. Wind a piece of ivy around the bottom of a candle as part of a binding spell. Place a couple of sprigs on your altar for spiritual journeys that take you inward as well as guide you out. Incorporate white ivy leaves into your esbat ritual as they are associated with the moon.

Ivy is associated with the elements air, earth, and water. Its astrological influence comes from the planet Saturn and the fixed star Alphecca. This plant is associated with fairies and the following deities: Arianrhod, Cernunnos, Danu, Dionysus, Frey, Hermes, Holle, Loki, Ogma, Osiris, Pan, Persephone, Rhea, and Saturn.

*Figure 31. Ivy is associated with the oghams Gort, Oir, and Uilleann (shown left to right).*

# In the Garden

## *Apple*

Modern Cultivated Apple (*Malus domestica* syn.
  *M. pumila, Pyrus pumila*)

Modern cultivated apple trees usually reach between fifteen and forty feet tall. Their short, crooked trunks are rough and fissured. The leaves are pointed and oval with finely serrated edges. They are yellowish green to dark green on top and pale, gray-green or whitish underneath. White to pinkish-white, five-petaled flowers are produced in clusters in the early spring. There are hundreds of modern apple cultivars.

While the crabapple is a favorite springtime tree with its stunning display of flowers (see the entry in "April"), the fruit of the modern cultivated apple is the essence of autumn. Although we can get apples year round from the supermarket, it's nice to have our favorite local variety through the winter. If you want to store apples, pick them just before they are ripe. A ripe apple stem will come away from the tree easily when you give the fruit a sharp twist. Choose apples that look ripe but have a little resistance to picking. Wrap each fruit in tissue or newspaper. Store them in an open box or tray in a cool, dry place. According to my grandmother, layering and covering the apples with maple leaves enhances the flavor by preventing them from absorbing odors. Of course, chanting and visualizing the apples surrounded by magical energy while picking and storing helps, too.

One of the easiest ways to incorporate the power of apples into magic work and rituals is to cut one horizontally to reveal the five-pointed star pattern. This apple pentagram has been called the star of knowledge. Place both halves of a cut apple on your altar to represent the Lord and Lady. For an esbat ritual, leave the apple whole but carve the triple moon symbol (waxing, full, waning) into the skin. Eating an apple before magic work helps access ancient wisdom. Wash and clean some apple seeds, and then make a circle with them around the base of a candle on your altar for fertility spells.

Following are two methods for love divination with apples: To find the initials of your true love, gently twist the stem of an apple and say a letter of the alphabet (starting with A) for each twist. The letter at which the stem breaks is the initial of the person's first name. Take the broken stem and poke it into the apple saying a letter at each poke. The letter at which the apple skin breaks is the initial of the person's surname. The other way of finding your true love's initials requires two apples. Carefully peel them, keeping the skin of each in one long strip. One at a time, throw them over your shoulders and then look for any initials formed by the peels.

The color of an apple can support magic work, too. Use a red apple for love, passion, and desires; a yellow/golden apple for success; and a green apple for abundance and prosperity. Also, burn a small piece of applewood to scent the home and attract abundance.

Apple is associated with the elements air and water. Its astrological influence comes from Venus. This tree is also associated with the following deities: Aphrodite, Apollo, Athena, Badb, Cailleach Bheur, Diana, Dionysus, Eros, Flora, Freya, Hera, Lugh, Macha, Manannan, Rhiannon, Venus, and Zeus.

*Figure 32. Apple is associated with the ogham Quert (left) and the rune Inguz (right).*

### Bistort

Common Bistort (*Persicaria bistorta* syn. *Polygonum bistorta*)
  *Also known as adderwort, dragonwort, meadow bistort, snakeroot, and snakeweed

Western Bistort (*Persicaria bistortoides* syn. *Polygonum bistortoides* )
  *Also known as American bistort, and snakeweed

Usually found in damp meadows or near water, common bistort forms large clumps of lance-shaped leaves. Resembling a bottlebrush, dense clusters of tiny white or pink flowers grow on spikes two to three feet tall. Western bistort is very similar with white flowers. As its name implies, it grows in western areas of North America. Both plants flower on and off from late spring to early autumn.

The common name bistort comes from the Latin *bis*, meaning "twice," and *torta*, "twisted," which describes the tangled, snakelike appearance of its roots.[91] In Scotland, the leaves were tied into a cloth and used to undo spells. In addition, bistort was used

---

91  D. C. Watts, *Dictionary of Plant Lore* (Oxford, England: Oxford University Press, 1997), 34.

medicinally for a wide range of ailments. Despite its depiction amongst plants that symbolize fertility in one of the famous unicorn tapestries—and its subsequent association with fertility and conception—bistort was actually used as an abortifacient.[92]

Sprinkle dried flowers and leaves around your ritual area for purification. Burn small pieces of root as you visualize the smoke removing whatever is unwanted from your life. Strew dried pieces of root in front of your home to repel negative energy. To increase psychic awareness, place leaves and/or flowers on your altar during ritual, divination, or other psychic practices.

Bistort is associated with the element earth. Its astrological influence comes from Saturn and the fixed star Sirius.

*Figure 33. Bistort is associated with the rune Nauthiz.*

## Maple
Sugar Maple (*Acer saccharum*)
　*Also known as bird's eye maple and hard maple

Well known for its fiery autumn colors, the sugar maple grows to a height of sixty to seventy-five feet, and it can spread forty to fifty feet wide at maturity. Its dark green leaves have three to five lobes and can reach a width of six inches. This tree produces clusters of small, greenish-yellow flowers in April and May. Pairs of winged seeds mature in September and October. Maple bark is rough and gray.

Maple's species name *saccharum*, means "sugary," which refers to the tree's sweet sap.[93] The folk name bird's eye maple refers to the eye-like patterns that are revealed when the wood is cut. The name hard maple comes from the hardness of its wood. In

---

92 Janet Farrell Brodie, *Contraception and Abortion in Nineteenth-century America* (Ithaca, NY: Cornell University Press, 1994), 42.

93 Coombes, *Dictionary of Plant Names*, 17.

Old English the maple was called a *mazer* or *maser* tree in reference to the name of a drinking bowl made from a large maple burl.[94]

If green leaves are still available, place one under a green candle on your altar to attract prosperity. Sprinkle dried red leaves as part of a spell to attract or rekindle love. Place a few winged maple seeds and dried leaves in a sachet and hang it on a bedpost to foster prophetic dreams. For esbat rituals, use seeds to make a circle on your altar with the seed ends touching each other and the wings pointing outward. Press a variety of colored leaves in a book, and then place them on your desk or workspace to boost creativity. Look for fallen maple branches as they make excellent wands.

Maple is associated with the elements air and earth. Its astrological influence comes from Jupiter. This tree is also associated with the goddesses Athena, Rhiannon, and Venus.

### Tansy

Common Tansy (*Tanacetum vulgare* syn. *Chrysanthemum vulgare*)
    *Also known as garden tansy, golden buttons, and yellow buttons

Growing from one to four feet tall, tansy is sometimes described as weedy because of its tendency to sprawl. Its deeply cut, fern-like leaves are aromatic. Clusters of flat, bright yellow flowers resemble buttons, or daisies without white petals. The flower's strong scent is long lasting, even when dried. Tansy arrived in North America in colonial times, escaped the domestic garden, and made itself at home along roadsides and fields.

The name tansy is a corruption of the Greek word *athanasia*, meaning "immortality."[95] The genus *Tanacetum* was the medieval Latin name for the plant. Tansy has a long history of use in folk medicine dating back to the ancient Greeks and Romans. However, most modern herbalists warn against its internal use by laypeople.

Dating to ancient times, tansy was put into coffins and tucked into funeral shrouds. Wreaths of it were also sometimes placed on the dead. Tansy continued to be used as part of funeral practices into the nineteenth century in New England. During the

---

94    Ernest Small, *North American Cornucopia: Top 100 Indigenous Food Plants* (Boca Raton, FL: CRC Press, 2014), 651.

95    Dobelis, *Magic and Medicine of Plants*, 318.

Middle Ages, tansy was used to treat a range of ailments. It did double duty as a strewing herb to freshen the air and control pests, and it was widely used in public places during the plague years.

Considered an antidote to black magic, place dried tansy flowers with your ritual and magic tools to repel negative energy. Hang small tufts of tansy above your altar or front door to repel negativity. Cut short sprigs and use them to "comb" and cleanse someone's aura or your own. Afterward, burn the sprigs and bury the ashes. Dry bunches of tansy flowers for use on your Samhain altar, or dry them any time a loved one passes as a blessing and offering to the dead.

Tansy is associated with the element water, and its astrological influence comes from Venus.

## In the Wild
### Goldenrod
European Goldenrod (*Solidago virgaurea*)
  *Also known as wound weed and woundwort

Sweet Goldenrod (*S. odora*)
  *Also known as blue mountain tea

These harbingers of autumn are clump-forming perennials. The European goldenrod grows three to seven feet tall with clusters of small flowers on spikes. Its lance-shaped leaves smell similar to Queen Anne's lace (*Daucus carota*) when crushed. Sweet goldenrod reaches two to four feet tall, and its lance-shaped leaves smell like anise when crushed. Its flower clusters grow on the upper sides of plume-like branches. Both plants bloom during August and September and can be found along roadsides and in open fields.

The genus name comes from the Latin *solida*, meaning "whole," and *ago*, "to make."[96] As this suggests, goldenrod has been used for a range of medicinal purposes. According to folklore, goldenrod points toward hidden treasure or hidden springs. It was also believed that carrying a piece of goldenrod would aid in finding treasure. Blooming at the same time as ragweed (*Ambrosia artemisiifolia*), goldenrod took the rap for causing hay fever until studies showed that its pollen is too heavy to be airborne.

---

96   Kowalchik and Hylton, *Rodale's Illustrated Encyclopedia of Herbs*, 230.

Use dried flowers in a sachet for spells to attract wealth and prosperity. Place several sprigs of flowers and leaves on your altar to aid in divination. Cut long stems of flower plumes and place these wherever you need to lift and boost energy.

Goldenrod is associated with the element air. Its astrological influence comes from Venus.

### Gravel Root/Joe Pye Weed

Sweet Joe-Pye Weed (*Eutrochium purpureum*)
   *Also known as gravelweed, jopi, purple boneset, meadowsweet, and queen of the meadow

Gravel root can reach five to seven feet tall and spread two to four feet wide. Its green, purple-tinged leaves are lance-shaped and coarsely serrated. They grow in whorls along the stem. Tiny pinkish-purple flowers grow in dome-shaped clusters and bloom from July to September. Seed heads stay on the plant into winter. The stems and flowers have a vanilla-like scent.

While there are many versions of the story about Joe Pye, the only consensus is that he was a medicine man in Colonial New England, and was said to have aided English settlers with Native American remedies from this plant. The name gravel root comes from its use for removing stones from the urinary tract. Gravel root is different from another plant called meadowsweet (*Filipendula ulmaria*), which is also known as queen of the meadow. That plant is covered in "June."

Carry a piece of dried root to bring luck and success. Make a sachet with leaves and flowers to include in your bath before a job interview or important meeting. Burn a small piece of dried root to dispel negative energy. Fresh flowers enhance visualizations and aid in making contact with the spirit realm as well as spirit guides.

Gravel root is associated with the element water.

## In the House

### Rosehips

A rosehip is the fruit of a rose, which is also known as a rose haw. The dog rose (*Rosa canina*), which is covered in "July," and the sweet briar rose (*Rosa rubiginosa* syn.

*R. eglanteria*) produce some of the best rosehips. The flowers must stay on the plant in order to produce the fruit. Wait for cool weather before collecting rosehips. At the time of harvest, hips should be firm but have a little give. Chant as you gather the rosehips to put magical energy into them.

Using a heavy-duty needle and darning thread, string rosehips together to make a circlet before drying them. Make a circlet large enough so when you lay it on your altar you can place things within the circle when doing magic work. Rosehips are especially supportive for clairvoyance. Alternatively, make a smaller circlet to wear as a bracelet when doing divination or psychic work. Also, hang it on your bedpost to enhance dream work. Use dried and crumbled rosehips to break hexes and in spells to banish unwanted things from your life. Carry a whole, dried rosehip to attract luck or provide protection.

### MAGICALLY HEALING ROSEHIP TEA

Rosehips are full of vitamin C and make a wonderful healing tea to have on hand for the winter. Gathering and preparing your own rosehips gives you the opportunity to infuse them with healing energy.

After giving them a good rinse with water, let the rosehips dry, and then cut off the ends. If you are drying a circlet of rosehips, don't cut off the ends. For making tea, cut the larger rosehips in half so they will dry faster. Lay them out in a single layer on a cookie sheet and place them on low heat in the oven with the door ajar. They will be hard and brittle when dry. Use a food processor to chop them into small pieces for tea. Place the pieces in a sieve and gently shake them. This gets rid of the little hairs that grow on the rosehips. Store in a jar with a tight-fitting lid out of direct light.

To make tea, put one to two teaspoons of rose hips in a mug and pour in a cup of boiling water. Cover and let it steep for about fifteen minutes, and then strain. Add a little honey to take away the tartness.

### Elderberries

In addition to rosehips and blackberries, this is the time to gather elderberries. The elder tree was covered in "June." Ripe elderberries are actually dark purple but appear light blue because of a slightly waxy coating. If you rub the berry, the coating comes off, revealing the darker color. Be sure to use only ripe ones because unripe elderberries can be toxic when consumed. Ripe berries can be frozen or dried.

Use elderberries in love charms for attraction and in spells to increase fidelity. Place a handful of berries on your altar during healing circles to support the energy. Use crumbled, dried berries in a sachet to enhance sleep and to encourage dreams.

### Elderberry Jam

4 cups fresh elderberries

3 cups sugar

Crush berries and combine with sugar. Stir over low heat until the sugar dissolves. Continue to let it simmer, stirring frequently. Test by placing a small amount on a plate. If it stays in place, it's done. While hot, pour into sterilized jars.

As you make the jam, chant:

*Lady of the woods, elder tree; bring your magic to each berry. Infuse them with love and healing sweet; in your honor I make this treat.*

# October

A mild breeze whispers on sunny afternoons, but nighttime comes earlier now as the harbingers of winter steal leaves from the trees. Moonlight shimmers on frosty ground and the earth prepares for sleep. October brings a strong sense of seasonal shift, summer becomes a fond memory, and we move toward the dark of the year. This month takes its name from the Latin *octo*, meaning "eight," as it was the eighth month on the Roman calendar.[97]

## On the Calendar
### October 28: The Celtic Month of Reed Begins
While reed does not seem like a prestigious enough plant to be ranked among trees, it was an extremely important component for warm, dry homes to the early people of the British Isles. Reed and its cousins are associated with health and healing, knowledge and learning, and one's unfolding destiny.

---

97  Payack, *A Million Words and Counting*, 176.

## Reed and Cattails

Common Reed (*Phragmites australis* syn. *Phragmites communis*)
   \*Also known as common reed grass, Dutch reed, and Norfolk reed
Cattails (*Typha latifolia*)
   \*Also known as cat-o-nine-tails, great reed mace, and water torch

Reed is a grass with round, hollow stems that can reach a height of thirteen feet. Its long, flat leaves are narrow and pointed. Plume-like flowers with tufts of silky hair grow on little spikelets in midsummer. After the leaves break away in autumn, a bare stem is left standing through the winter. Cattails can grow four to eight feet tall and also have flat, blade-like leaves. Its dense, brown, cylindrical flowering spike stays on the plant through autumn before breaking up into downy, white fluff. These plants are found in marshy, wet areas.

Reed and cattails have provided material for roof thatching, arrow shafts, musical instruments, and many other domestic items. Reeds and cattails are cousins, sharing the same order, *Poales*, but different families and genera. The genus name for reed, *Phragmites*, comes from Greek and means "growing in hedges" or "fence-like," which describes its appearance of creating a thick barrier.[98] The genus name for cattails, *Typha*, also comes from Greek and means "bog" or "marsh."[99]

Place several long stalks of cattails in a tall vase in your bedroom to enhance passion and sex, especially if there are issues in a relationship. For protection in ritual or spell work, cut six equal lengths of reed to lay out in two triangles to form a pentagram on your altar. Stalks of reed or cattails on your altar will help you to connect with ancestors. Burn a piece of reed to honor any household spirit as well as to bring unity and loyalty to your family. Pull apart a cattail flower spike to make a protection sachet/amulet that you wear during journeys to other realms. Hang it above your altar when doing magic work.

Reed and cattails are associated with the element water. Reed's astrological influence comes from Mars and Pluto, and cattails' from Mars.

---

98   Sylvan T. Runkel and Dean M. Roosa, *Wildflowers and Other Plants of Iowa Wetlands, Second Edition* (Iowa City, IA: Iowa State University Press, 2014), 207.

99   *Ibid.*, 105.

Figure 34. Reed is associated with the ogham Ngetal (left) and the rune Algiz (right).

### October 31: Samhain

Samhain is a time to remember ancestors and invite their spirits to come close. Legends of evil spirits on the prowl this night are misunderstandings of the belief that the barrier between the worlds of the seen and unseen is thin. It was the custom in parts of Europe to place candles in windows to help ancestors find their way. This eventually developed into the jack-o'-lantern, which was intended to welcome and guide spirits to the home, and to warn any unwanted ones to stay away.

It was customary to celebrate and hold a feast for the dead on Samhain. The feast could be a complete meal with an extra place set for those not physically present, or it could be as simple as leaving cakes and wine by the fireside or on the front step. Samhain has also been a night for divination using nuts, especially hazelnuts, as these were believed to hold ancient wisdom.

Decorate your altar with carved pumpkins, chrysanthemums, marigolds, and bittersweet. Let the power of the green world aid you in opening the portal between the worlds and connecting with loved ones who have passed. I like to include a piece of chocolate on my altar to symbolize my wish that my loved ones enjoy a sweet passage through the afterlife.

## In the Garden
### Belladonna Lily

(*Amaryllis belladonna* syn. *Callicore rosea*)
   *Also known as autumn amaryllis, magic lily, naked lady,
   and rain lily

The belladonna lily produces flat, strap-like leaves in late autumn that die back in the spring. Beginning in late summer, naked stems emerge from which two to twelve trumpet-shaped flowers grow. The sweetly scented flowers are white, pink, or slightly purple. Although the belladonna lily blooms in late summer, there is great variation in how late into the autumn the flowers last. Those of us in more northern areas can grow the belladonna lily as a potted plant that is taken indoors for the winter.

While this plant is poisonous and should not be ingested, the word belladonna in its name does not mean that it is related to the deadly nightshade belladonna (*Atropa belladonna*). The word belladonna is Italian, meaning "beautiful lady," which is a reference to the flushed pink color of the belladonna lily's flowers.

This plant is easily confused with its strikingly similar cousin, the resurrection lily (*Lycoris squamigera*), which shares many of its common names. The belladonna lily is actually the only species in the *Amaryllis* genus. The plant commonly called amaryllis, with which many of us are familiar, is the indoor bulb (*Hippeastrum* spp.) popular around the winter holidays. Although it is not a true amaryllis, it looks similar to the belladonna lily. Refer to that plant's entry in "January."

Place three belladonna lily flowers on your altar during full or new moon rituals to call on the beauty of Luna. Dry several flowers and use them in sachets for love charms. Dried flowers can also be used to break a love spell.

Holding a flower, circle your ritual space three times to consecrate and purify the area. Like most lilies, this one is a flower of renewal, especially since it arises from the ground on its own—unaccompanied by leaves. Place a vase of these flowers on your altar to aid in transitions or to initiate a new phase of your life.

The belladonna lily is associated with the element water, and its astrological influence comes from the moon.

### Chrysanthemum

Common Chrysanthemum (*Chrysanthemum morifolium* syn.
 *Dendranthema grandiflorum, Anthemis grandiflora*)
 *Also known as garden mum and mum

This well-known perennial continues to bring color to the garden long after most other plants have faded. Reaching one to three feet tall, chrysanthemums have dark green, deeply lobed leaves. Their dense flower heads can be white, yellow, orange, or reddish-orange, as well as various shades of purple. The thirteen classes of chrysanthemums are based on flower form.

Chrysanthemums were first cultivated by the Chinese approximately 1500 BCE.[100] In Chinese art and folklore, these flowers were a symbol of marital bliss. Although the chrysanthemum represented the sun and life in Japan, this flower was used to honor the dead in France, Italy, and Germany. It became known as *Fiori dei Morte*, "flower of the dead."[101] Despite this, the flower was a symbol of cheerfulness and optimism to the Victorians.

Planted outside in a garden or indoors as a potted plant, chrysanthemums bring blessings and protection to the home. Use a red flower in love charms, a white one on your altar when seeking truth, and a yellow one to aid in recovering from slighted love. Remove the petals from a flower and scatter them across a stream or pond as you visualize releasing unwanted things from your life. Float intact flower heads in a large bowl of water when seeking forgiveness. A couple can give the flowers to one another in a handfasting ritual to represent their love and commitment.

If you use chrysanthemums on your Samhain altar, leave them in place until November 2, as they are also associated with All Soul's Day.

Chrysanthemum is associated with the element fire. Its astrological influence comes from the sun.

### Haws/Hawthorn Berries
*Also known as pixie paws

Commonly known as haws, hawthorn berries ripen at this time year. These oval, red berries were used medicinally by the ancient Greeks but seemed to fall out of favor until the nineteenth century in England. In "May," we learned what to do with the leaves and blossoms. Refer to that chapter for more details about the hawthorn tree. Let's see what magic we can do with the fruit.

Place a white candle on your altar and surround the base of it with a ring of haws to aid in fertility spells. Also called pixie paws, haws are instrumental in attracting pixies, fairies, and other nature spirits to a garden. Place a few on your outdoor altar along with a trinket for them. Line a kitchen windowsill with haws to attract prosperity. Also, this

---

100   Cumo, *Encyclopedia of Cultivated Plants*, 266.

101   Kear, *Flower Wisdom*, 116.

fruit can be used in spells for defensive magic and to repel negativity. Lay out a group of haws in the pattern of the ogham Huath or the rune Othila to call on the energy of the hawthorn.

*Figure 35. The Hawthorn tree is associated with the ogham Huath (left) and the rune Othila (right).*

### Marigold
African Marigold (*Tagetes erecta* syn. *T. major*)
  *Also known as American marigold, Aztec marigold, big marigold, and chrysanthemum marigold

French Marigold (*T. patula*)

The African marigold reaches one to four feet in height. Its large, rounded flowers are various shades of yellow, whitish, or orange, and its lance-shaped leaves are coarsely toothed. The French marigold is a compact plant that grows only six to twelve inches tall. It has toothed, lance-shaped leaflets. In varying yellows, oranges, and reds, its flowers can be single or double. Both of these aromatic marigolds are annuals that bloom from June until frost arrives. These should not be confused with plants in the genus *Calendula*, which are also called marigolds. Those plants have flowers that are more like daisies.

Although the marigold originated in South America, its botanical name honors the Roman god Tages, grandson of Jupiter. According to legend, Tages taught humans about agriculture and how to plow fields. Considered the flower of the dead by the Aztecs, marigolds are used on altars for Day of the Dead observances (November 2) in present-day Mexico.

As a symbol of pain and grief, it was a custom to place marigolds in a vase with roses to symbolize the sweet sorrows of love. Marigolds also represented constancy in love and were used in bridal bouquets. According to folklore, holding a bouquet of these flowers aids in seeing fairies. In addition, the color of marigolds was said to ward off witches.

Marigolds can help clarify your purpose in a divination session. Hold a couple of leaves between your hands, and then place them on your altar while you proceed with your reading. Also do this to aid in developing psychic skills. Use the flowers on your altar at Samhain, or any time a loved one passes as a blessing and offering to the dead. Associated with success, marigold leaves can be an aid in legal matters by supporting a determined mind. Use flowers and leaves in spells to attract abundance, comfort, and happiness to the home. Make a dream pillow with dried flower petals to invite prophetic dreams; place the pillow under the bed to ease nightmares.

Marigold is associated with the elements air and fire. Its astrological influence comes from the sun and the fixed star Procyon. This flower is also associated with fairies.

### Pumpkin

Field Pumpkin (*Cucurbita pepo* var. *pepo*)

The familiar orange pumpkin is actually a variety of a plant that also produces yellow crookneck squash (var. *torticollia*), zucchini (var. *cylindrica*), acorn squash (var. *turbinata*), and others. In addition, there are many cultivars that provide a wide range of shapes, sizes, and colors of pumpkins. *Cucurbita* is Latin for "gourd" and *pepo*, "melon." The latter may have been derived from the Greek *pepon*, meaning "ripe."[102]

The thick, winding, branching pumpkin vine can grow more than fifteen feet long. The rounded leaves have deeply cut lobes and serrated edges. Large, bright yellow or orange, trumpet-shaped flowers start blooming in July. The pumpkins ripen in September and October. If they have a hollow sound when thumped, they are ready to harvest.

It is believed that pumpkins originated in Central America about 7,500 years ago.[103] Early European explorers took the curious-looking fruit back to the Old World. By the time the Pilgrims set foot in Plymouth, they were already familiar with pumpkins. Originating as a carved turnip, the jack-o'-lantern found a more impressive medium in the larger pumpkin.

---

102   Small, *North American Cornucopia*, 663.

103   Andrew F. Smith, *Food and Drink in American History: A "Full Course" Encyclopedia, Volume 1: A-L* (Santa Barbara, CA: ABC-CLIO, LLC, 2013), 726.

In the past, dreaming of a pumpkin was regarded as a bad omen. It was also believed to indicate that witchcraft was being used against you or a trick was being played on you.

When carving a pumpkin for Samhain, don't throw out the pulpy goop. Sort through it and save the seeds because they also serve as magical tools. There's no way around making a mess, so just place the pulp in a colander, rinse with water, and then start picking out the seeds. If you have a second colander, use that to hold the seeds because they will need further rinsing. Afterwards, lay the seeds out on a paper towel to dry, which will take about a week. Alternatively, dry them on a baking sheet in the oven with the temperature set as low as possible for three or four hours. Stir them frequently to keep them from singeing.

As a symbol of abundance, pumpkins can be used to draw prosperity to your home. Place three small pumpkins on a kitchen windowsill or table during the autumn season. As you do this, say three times:

*May wealth, health, and love abound; in this house and all around.*

After Samhain, bury the pumpkins in the ground.

Like reading tea leaves, a handful of pumpkin seeds can be used for divination. First, hold them between your hands as you visualize your question or whatever you seek guidance for. Toss them into the air, and then look for patterns or symbols that they may form on the floor.

Make a circle with seeds on your altar for an esbat ritual or when working with moon magic to draw the power of Luna. When blowing out the candle inside a pumpkin, place an index finger in front of your mouth as you blow, and make a wish.

Pumpkin is associated with the element earth, and its astrological influence comes from the moon.

## In the Wild
### Bittersweet
American Bittersweet (*Celastrus scandens*)
  *Also known as false bittersweet

European Bittersweet (*Solanum dulcamara*)
  *Also known as bitter nightshade, climbing nightshade, woody
  nightshade, and violet-bloom

American bittersweet is a perennial woody vine with clusters of greenish-white flowers that bloom from May to June. Its pointed, oval leaves are yellowish-green. In the autumn, the round, red berry is surrounded by a "jacket" that looks like yellow-orange petals. American bittersweet is found in wooded areas, thickets, and rocky slopes.

European bittersweet is a perennial vine with woody lower stems. The leaves are dark-green and deeply lobed with a large, arrow-shaped center lobe and two small lobes at its base. The star-shaped flower has a prominent, yellow cone at the center and purple, backward-arching petals. Blooming for several months during the summer, the flowers give way to round berries. The berries start out green, and then change color to yellow, then orange, and finally red. This does not happen all at once and you may find the full range of colored berries on a single plant. European bittersweet is found in backyards, edges of fields, vacant lots, and roadsides. The leaves are just as toxic as the berries if ingested.

The species name *dulcamara* for European bittersweet refers to the flavor of the berries that are first bitter and then sweet.[104] It is said to be an unpleasant sweetness and certainly not worth the risk to find out, as it can be deadly. The berries of American bittersweet are also toxic when ingested. Always handle any parts of these plants with care.

Write the name of something or someone you no longer want in your life on a piece of paper. Wrap three bittersweet berries in the paper, put it in a box for three weeks, and then take the paper and berries outside to burn and bury. Bittersweet can also be used in this way to remove spells and hexes. On Samhain, place a sprig or two of dried berries on your altar to represent the bitter sweet sorrow in remembering loved ones who have passed to the other side of the veil.

Bittersweet is associated with the element air and the goddess Hecate. Its astrological influence comes from Mercury, Pluto, and Saturn.

### Burdock
Greater Burdock (*Arctium lappa*)
   *Also known as billy buttons, bur, burweed, and cockle buttons

---

104   Dobelis, *Magic and Medicine of Plants*, 103.

Growing six to eight feet tall, greater burdock is a biennial with purplish, grooved stems. Its elongated, heart-shaped leaves are dull green with wavy edges. Clusters of purple, thistle-like flowers bloom from July to October. The spiky round seedpods called burs turn brown and remain on the plant until they get attached to passing animals or people. The burs are said to have been the inspiration for the invention of Velcro. This plant is called greater burdock because it has a smaller cousin called lesser burdock (*A. minus*). Burdock is found along roadsides, in fields, and in waste areas.

The ancient Greeks called burdock *arcteion*, which was derived from *arktos*, "bear."[105] The bent hooks on the burs are said to resemble coarse bear fur. The common name burdock comes from the French *burre*, meaning a " bur," and the Old English *doc*, meaning "large leaf."[106] Although they are somewhat similar in appearance, burdock should not be confused with the toxic common cocklebur (*Xanthium strumarium*).

Wearing a costume covered in burs, the Burry Man was part of an old village tradition in England. In some areas this practice was associated with harvest festivals. Occasionally accompanied by attendants, the Burry Man paraded around village streets. While the origin of this custom is unknown, one theory is that this character was a form of the Green Man representing the spirit of vegetation. Another theory is that the Burry Man walked the village to symbolically catch evil in his burs and carry it away.

According to folklore, burdock leaves were used in love potions to stimulate lust. They were also used in a form of divination to tell if someone had a sweetheart. A bur tossed at a person's back that stuck to his or her clothing was an affirmative answer.

Wearing gloves and a hat for protection, walk to an area where burdock grows. Carefully place three burs on the top of your head. Continue on your walk as you think of things you want to remove from your life or things that you fear. After doing this, remove the burs and roll them between your hands to break them up. Throw the pieces to the wind as you say:

*Be gone, be gone, from my life be gone.*

---

105   Wood, *The Book of Herbal Wisdom*, 138.
106   *Ibid.*

Collect four burs and keep them intact. Place one at each corner of your house for protection. Burs and/or leaves can be used in defensive magic to ward off negativity. Also, grind a dried piece of root, and then sprinkle it in a circle to purify your ritual space.

Burdock is associated with the element water. Its astrological influence comes from the planet Venus and the fixed star Ala Corvi.

### Evening Primrose
(*Oenothera biennis*)
   *Also known as evening star, king's cure all, night light,
   and night willow herb

This prairie wildflower has a rosette of large basal leaves and an erect stem that can reach three to six feet tall. Lance-shaped leaves with wavy edges grow on the same stems with flowers. At dusk, the shiny yellow flowers unfurl and perfume the air. Blooming a few at a time, these four-petaled flowers are two inches wide and last only one night. The flowers give way to clusters of oblong seed capsules.

Although not a true primrose, it was so named because of its resemblance to the small common primrose (*Primula vulgaris* syn. *P. acaulis*). The folk name night light comes from the slight phosphorescence of the blossoms that emit a faint light.

Native Americans used the roots for a medicinal tea and various other parts of the plant for other remedies. English settlers used the lemon-scented leaves as a culinary herb. Evening primrose was taken back to Europe where it has become naturalized. This plant is popular in modern herbal medicine.

Evening primrose is a powerful support for magic. Place a couple of flowers on your altar to boost the energy of spells. Cut a stalk, let it dry, and then use it as a wand for banishing spells. Place a dried stalk in the attic or a place high in your house to invite protection and foster a sense of safety. Hold a leaf between your palms for help in finding truth while you meditate on a situation. As a healer, evening primrose provides balance during times of change. To commemorate a new beginning, burn a dried leaf in your cauldron.

Evening primrose is associated with the element fire, and its astrological influence comes from Venus.

## Locust

Honey Locust (*Gleditsia triacanthos*)

　*Also known as sweet locust, thorn tree, and thorny locust

Black Locust (*Robinia pseudoacacia*)

　*Also known as false acacia and yellow locust

The honey locust reaches thirty-five to seventy-five feet tall. Its leaves are comprised of seven to nineteen oval leaflets that turn yellow in autumn. Inconspicuous greenish-white flowers bloom in May and June. Long, flat, twisted seedpods form in late summer and turn from yellow-green to reddish-brown. These stay on the tree into winter. Growing to a length of six inches or more, dark reddish thorns with three or more points form on the trunk and branches. The species name, *triacanthos*, comes from Greek and means "three-thorn."[107]

The black locust is about the same size and has very similar leaves to the honey locust. Its white flowers grow in pendulous clusters that can be four to eight inches long. It also develops seedpods; however, these are straight rather than twisted. Unlike the impressive thorns of the honey locust, pairs of small sharp spines grow along the branches at the leaf axils. The word black in its name refers to the tree's dark-colored bark and seedpods. Its leaves turn yellow in autumn. The seedpods of the black locust are poisonous to humans.

To stimulate protective energy, place a large thorn from a honey locust or several spines from a black locust on a windowsill pointing in the direction from which you feel a threat. Place them under your front porch to repel negativity from your home. Locust tree thorns and spines can also be used in spells to increase perseverance and determination when working to overcome obstacles. Burn a few dried leaves to seal a binding spell. Use dried, intact seedpods as rattles for dark moon rituals. Any part of the tree, especially the thorns and spines, aids in connecting with dark goddesses.

Locust is associated with the elements earth and water. The goddesses Cerridwen, Hecate, the Morrigan, and Sekhmet are also associated with this tree.

---

107　Raymond L. Taylor, *Plants of Colonial Days* (Mineola, NY: Dover Publications Inc., 1996), 49.

### Queen Anne's Lace
(*Daucus carota*)

*Also known as bird's nest weed, devil's plague, and wild carrot

Introduced into North America from Europe, Queen Anne's lace is a familiar sight in fields, ditches, and open areas. Growing one to four feet tall, it has feathery leaves and wide, flat umbels of tiny white flowers that bloom from May to October. Each umbel has a dark reddish-purple floret at the center. After its seeds set, the umbel curls up and inward, forming a cup that resembles a bird's nest.

Be careful not to confuse Queen Anne's lace with the poisonous water hemlock (*Cicuta maculata*) and fool's parsley (*Aethusa cynapium*). The distinguishing feature of Queen Anne's lace is the reddish-purple spot at the center of the flower head.

The root, which is much smaller than today's cultivated carrot, was a common food in ancient Greece and Rome. In the Middle Ages it was believed that the boiled flowers could be used for a love potion. In the sixteenth century Queen Anne's lace was introduced into Great Britain, where the flowers and leaves became popular hair accessories. This plant's common name comes from the story that Queen Anne of England (1665–1714) pricked her finger while sewing and a drop of blood landed in the center of her white lace. Finding this plant almost impossible to remove from fields because of its deep root, farmers called it devil's plague.

Make an infusion of leaves and add it to a purification bath before performing spells for love, fertility, or virility. If any flowers are still available, use them to decorate your altar for attraction spells as well as esbat rituals, or use the leaves and "birds nest" seed heads. Also use the seed heads in spells to increase fertility. Wrap a dried root in lace and put it under your pillow to enhance dream work or to encourage prophetic dreams.

## In the House
### Sloes

Sloes are the fruit of the blackthorn tree (*Prunus spinosa*), which was covered in "May." These are often the last fruit to be harvested, as it is best to wait until after the first few frosts to gather sloes. Frost softens the skin of the fruit and makes for a better flavor. Adding the flavor of sloes to gin makes a nice winter drink for the holidays.

................

## Sloe Gin

2 pounds sloes

4–6 ounces sugar

Gin

After washing, prick each sloe with a fork. Place them in a large jar with the sugar. Use a jar large enough so this fills it halfway. Fill the rest of the jar with gin, and close tightly. Store for two or three months giving the jar a good shake occasionally. Strain out the fruit and bottle the gin. Keep the strained-out fruit to use for dessert toppings on ice cream, cheesecake, or whatever appeals to your taste buds. Also, the strained fruit can be frozen until needed.

Of course, in addition to flavoring gin, sloes can be used to give strength to spells. They can be dried and used as amulets for protection or to help gain control of a situation.

# November

November is a time that is betwixt and between. After passing through the gateway of Samhain, we have come into the dark of the year. As the days grow cold and the nights long, we await the rebirth of light at Yule. Although the earth begins her winter's rest, there are quiet reminders of ongoing life. November is named from the Latin *novem*, meaning "nine," as it was the ninth month on the Roman calendar.[108]

## On the Calendar
### *November 1 and 2: Day of the Dead/All Saints Day and All Soul's Day*
The days following Samhain continue to be important for honoring the dead and purifying for the future. Like many spiritually important observances, these were adapted into the Christian calendar. On All Soul's Day, it was common practice to place chrysanthemums on the graves of loved ones. See "October" for details on this flower.

---

108     Payack, *A Million Words and Counting*, 176.

Until the eighteenth century in England, fires of gorse were lit to lead departed souls to their former homes.[109]

............

## GORSE

Common Gorse (*Ulex europaeus*)
  *Also known as broom, furze, golden gorse, prickly bloom, and whin

Gorse is a spiny evergreen shrub that reaches five feet tall and wide. Its densely packed branches are prickly with half-inch spines that grow amongst the leaves. The gray-green leaves resemble spruce needles and are shorter than the spines. Gorse was introduced into North America as an ornamental hedge plant, but its invasive nature caused it to fall out of favor. Although it produces a profusion of bright yellow, pea-like flowers in the spring and early summer, it often blooms throughout the year. The flowers grow singly or in pairs.

Folklore from various countries indicates that gorse was an effective plant to use against fairy mischief. Dreaming of gorse means that good fortune is on the way. Picking the flowers in your dream indicates prosperity. In Ireland where gorse blooms year round, a sprig in a bridal bouquet alluded to the saying that kissing was out of fashion only when the whin was out of blossom. However, in England, giving someone gorse blossoms was considered unlucky because it would make people quarrel. In some areas of England, children were afraid to pick the flowers or go near the bushes because it was believed that dragons lived or were born in gorse thickets. Called fuzz moots, gorse roots were dried and burned as fuel.

The name furze was derived from *fyrs*, the Anglo-Saxon name for the plant.[110] It is sometimes called broom because it is similar in appearance and is often confused with the plant more commonly called broom (*Cytisus scoparius*).

For protection spells, carve its associated ogham character on a yellow candle and place gorse sprigs around the base of it. Place gorse spines at each corner of your altar for defense against dark magic and for help to remove hexes. Bury a sprig of gorse in front of your house for protection. If you find a bush that is in bloom, use the flowers in

---

109   Jones and Deer, *The Country Diary of Garden Lore*, 103.
110   Grieve, *A Modern Herbal*, 368.

love sachets or scatter a few in your bath to increase personal power for magic. Burn a few leaves and/or spines for help in getting out of a rut. Place a sprig or two in any area of your home where energy has stagnated. Use gorse branches to symbolically sweep your altar and ritual area, cleaning and clearing the way for the sun's return at Yule.

Gorse is associated with the element fire. Its astrological influence comes from Mars and the sun. This plant is also associated with the deities Aine, Arianrhod, Belenus, the Dagda, Freyr, Lugh, Jupiter, and Thor.

*Figure 36. Gorse is associated with the ogham Onn.*

### *November 11: Lunantishees*

This is one of the days that blackthorn trees should not be cut. Lunantishees were believed to be a tribe of fairies and guardians of these trees. See the entry in "May" for more information about blackthorn and the Lunantishees. To honor these fairies on this day, tie a black ribbon around the trunk of a blackthorn tree and wish them well.

### *November 25: The Celtic Month of Elder Begins*

Although it is not in bloom or fruiting, the elder is celebrated at this time of year because it is a tree of the Crone. In many areas, an old female spirit was believed to call the elder tree home. In Germany this spirit was known as Dame Ellhorn. In England, cutting down an elder without asking for the Crone's permission was considered very unwise due to negative consequences. Elder trees were also associated with witches, and planting one near your house was believed to aid in seeing them. See the entry in "June" for more information on this tree.

To find out if you are permitted to take a branch, stand in front of an elder tree and close your eyes. Hold your hands in front of you with your palms facing the elder as you reach out toward it with your energy. When you can sense the tree's energy, ask the Crone if you may take a branch.

If you may, place it on your altar at home to represent her through the dark of the year. It will help you call on her wisdom and power. At Yule, return the branch to the tree and place it on the ground underneath. If you do not have an elder tree in your area or did not sense an affirmative answer from Dame Ellhorn, carve elder's associated ogham and/or rune into a brown taper candle. Light it every third night until Yule. Spend time in meditation with the Crone as she beckons: "*Come into the darkness, explore what lies within.*"

Don't feel discouraged if you did not receive permission to take an elder branch. It may mean that you are not ready to work with the energy of the Crone through this tree. Spend time in the presence of an elder tree to open yourself to its energy. When the time is right, the Crone will let you know.

*Figure 37. Elder is associated with the ogham Ruis (left) and the rune Fehu (right).*

## In the Garden
### Heath and Heather
Common Heather (*Calluna vulgaris*)
   *Also known as Scotch heather

Hybrid Heath (*Erica* × *darleyensis*)

Winter Heath (*E. carnea* syn. *E. herbacea*)
   *Also known as spring heath and winter flowering heather

Although heath and heather are nearly identical and the names are often used interchangeably, there is a simple way to tell them apart. Heath has needle-like foliage (think spruce tree) while heather has tiny, scale-like foliage (think cedar tree). Also, common heather is the only species in the *Calluna* genus.

Common heather grows in mounds from four to twenty inches tall. Depending on the variety, its bell-shaped flowers can be white, pink, purple, or red. Heather usually flowers from summer to late autumn, but it can bloom into December. The heaths also have bell-shaped flowers. Their needle-like foliage grows in whorls along the branches. Hybrid heath's flower colors range from white to rosy. They bloom from November to April in mounds that can reach two feet tall. Winter heath can begin blooming as early as November with some varieties lasting through May. It typically grows in mounds six to nine inches tall.

In the past, both heath and heather were used for thatching roofs and making brooms. It had a wide range of other domestic uses including medicinal remedies. The flowers of common heather were used in a popular home brew called heather ale. The white variety of heather was considered a good luck charm and tucked into bridal bouquets.

The genus name *Calluna* comes from similar Latin and Greek words that have the same meaning of "brushing" or "sweeping."[111] This is in reference to heather plants being bundled together and used as brooms.

Make a sachet using white flowers for a good luck charm. White and/or pink flowers placed on the altar for three days strengthens love spells. Place a sprig with purple flowers on your altar to foster a deeper connection with your spirit guides. Burn a few dried sprigs to invite clarity and awareness while developing psychic abilities. Burning heather and heath also supports spiritual healing. A sprig of heather or heath hung on a bedpost or placed on a nightstand enhances dream work and helps in interpreting messages. Grow heather or heath in your garden to aid in protecting your home.

Both heather and heath are associated with the element water, and their astrological influence comes from Venus. In addition to fairies, they are associated with the goddesses Arianrhod, Isis, and Venus.

*Figure 38. Heather is associated with the ogham Ur.*

## Jasmine

Winter Jasmine (*Jasminum nudiflorum*)
   *Also known as yellow jasmine

Winter jasmine is a scrambling, spreading shrub that grows about four feet tall. Its arching branches take root where they touch the ground. Jasmine is often grown on a

---

111   Mario Molinari, *Divided by Words: Making a Case for a New Literacy* (Bury St. Edmonds, England: Arena Books, 2009), 32.

trellis. The bright yellow, tubular flowers have six petals and grow along the branches from November to March. Small leaves develop in the early spring. The species name, *nudiflorum*, comes from Latin, meaning "naked flower," in reference to the stems that remain bare of leaves when the plant is in bloom.[112]

Winter jasmine is easy to confuse with forsythia when they are both in bloom in the early spring; however, jasmine's flowers last several months whereas forsythia's are gone within two weeks. Unlike its white-flowered cousin, which is often referred to as summer jasmine (*J. grandiflorum*), winter jasmine is not fragrant.

Use jasmine flowers to boost defensive magic, enhance divination, and aid in contact with the spirit realm. Make a sachet of dried flowers for protection during dream work, channeling, or astral travel. The flowers will also enhance the depth of your dreams. Drape several trailing branches over your altar to help manifest desires. Place a small bowl or cup of dried flowers in your work area to stimulate ideas.

Spiritually, jasmine enhances intuition and brings inspiration for creative endeavors as well as clarity for communication. Burn dried flowers in spells to attract luck and prosperity as well as to bind a pledge. Place a ring of flowers around the base of a yellow candle on your altar to increase psychic skills. Burning the flowers or a small twig aids in releasing fears. A jasmine bush on your property will attract abundance and peace.

Jasmine is associated with the elements air, earth, and water. Its astrological influence comes from Mercury and the moon. This plant is also associated with the goddesses Diana and Rhiannon.

### Juniper
Common Juniper (*Juniperus communis*)
   *Also known as gin berry, hackmatack, horse savin, and savin

Juniper is a spreading evergreen that usually grows four to six feet tall. The bark is brown to reddish-brown. The juniper's foliage consists of needles in sets of three that grow in whorls along the branches. While young plants have needle-like leaves, mature ones have scale-like foliage, though some cultivars keep the same type of leaves all their

---

112   Gil Nelson, *Atlantic Coastal Plain Wildflowers* (Guilford, CT: The Globe Pequot Press, 2006), 84.

lives. Like holly, juniper has male and female flowers on separate plants and you need one of each type of bush if you want berries. Blooming from April to June, the male flowers are yellow and the female, yellowish-green. Both are inconspicuous and grow in groups of three at the base of the needles.

The round berries come from female flowers and are technically considered a cone. Taking about two years to mature, the berries turn from green to blue-black and frequently have a dusting of white powder covering them. Juniper berries are well known for their use as flavoring in stews and roasts, and especially gin. They are also used medicinally and for making an essential oil that is used in perfumes, soaps, and cosmetics.

According to folklore, burning juniper during childbirth would keep fairies from substituting a changeling for the baby. During the Middles Ages, juniper was burned as protection against the plague. In parts of England, it was believed that a person who cut down a juniper bush would die within the year. In Italy, branches were hung over doorways to frighten witches away. It was also believed that juniper could be planted in front of a house as protection against witches, who were (for some inexplicable reason) expected to count all the needles on the tree before they could pass through the doorway.

Burn dried needles as incense to purify a large space or to ward off the energy of negative people. Also burn juniper for defensive magic, as it is especially effective against black magic, hexes, and dealing with unwanted spirits. Use dried berries in a sachet to enhance divination and dream work. The berries also help increase psychic abilities. Burning any part of juniper strengthens psychic protection as it keeps energy grounded in the physical world. String berries together into a circlet, let the fruit dry out, and then use it as an amulet to attract a lover. A juniper bush on your property is effective for manifesting abundance and prosperity. As an offering, tie three small dark-blue ribbons within the thick foliage of a bush as you say:

*With branches of green and berries of blue; beautiful juniper, I thank you.*

Juniper is associated with the elements earth, fire, and water. Its astrological influence comes from Mars, Mercury, the moon, the sun, and the fixed star Sirius. It is also associated with the deities Balder, Holle, Loki, and the Morrigan.

*Figure 39. Juniper is associated with the rune Sowelu.*

## In the Wild

### Chickweed

Common Chickweed (*Stellaria media*)

　\*Also known as bird weed, passerina, satinflower, starweed,
　　tongue grass, and winterweed

Found in meadows, pastures, gardens, and lawns, this lanky, delicate annual has sprawling, tangled stems, which create a dense mat that can extend more than two feet. Its small, oval to egg-shaped leaves grow in pairs. A row of tiny hairs runs along one side of the stem to the first pair of leaves then switches to the other side of the stem. It switches back and forth from side to side at each set of leaves. The tiny star-shaped flowers are white with five petals that are deeply divided, giving the appearance of ten petals. These grow at the end of the stems and bloom from March to December. In mild areas, chickweed can bloom all year.

Chickweed flowers open on sunny days but close in the rain or when the sky is overcast. This was the basis of weather divination indicating no rain for at least four hours when the flowers were wide open. If they are shut, it will soon rain. The flowers develop into oval seed capsules.

After being ignored by ancient herbalists, chickweed became popular for a wide range of remedies in the Middle Ages. Although the leaves are tiny, they have been used as salad greens and cooked like spinach. Today, the use of chickweed by herbalists is limited.

This plant was named chickweed because chickens and other birds are fond of the seeds. In addition, the seeds were customarily given to caged birds. This plant's name passerina is also the name of a genus of birds in the cardinal family.

Dry several sprigs of leaves and flowers for a sachet to carry with you when you want to attract love. Place a sachet under your bed to increase fertility and foster fidelity in a relationship. Sprinkle flowers in your bath water to release negative feelings and anger. Burn a small amount of dried leaves and/or flowers to dispel negative energy in the home.

Place sprigs on your altar to bolster moon magic or enhance the energy of esbat rituals. Hold a sprig in each hand to draw down lunar energy. Chickweed adds strength to animal magic, and of course, when working with birds.

Chickweed is associated with the element water, and its astrological influence comes from the moon.

### Yew
American Yew (*Taxus canadensis*)
    *Also known as Canadian yew
English Yew (*T. baccata*)
    *Also known as common yew
Western Yew (*T. brevifolia*)
    *Also known as Pacific yew

Rarely over five feet tall, the American yew is an evergreen shrub with multiple stems and reddish bark. The English and Western yews are also evergreens; however, they can reach almost fifty feet tall. They both have dark green, needle-like leaves. Although they appear to grow from two sides of the branches, the needles are actually attached in spirals around the branches. The needles of the English yew are glossy on top, gray to pale green underneath. Yews produce seeds surrounded by a fleshy, red coating that looks like a cup-shaped berry. The seeds ripen from September to November and are toxic, as is the foliage. Native to North America, the American and Western yews are found in forests. A favorite for trimming into topiary shapes, the English yew was imported as a garden plant.

The yew can live for thousands of years and became a symbol of everlasting life. It is also associated with death and the afterlife perhaps because the seeds, bark, and leaves are poisonous. In England, yews were commonly planted in graveyards symbolizing death and resurrection. In addition to arrows and spears, yew wood was used for a wide range of votive objects in Britain, France, and Switzerland. Native Americans of the Pacific Northwest carved sacred ceremonial objects from the Western yew.

One particular yew in Devon, England, was for some unknown reason linked with fertility. According to legend, if a man walked backward and a woman forward around the tree, they would have children. Also, walking around the tree seven times was said to make a wish come true.

Place sprigs with berries on your altar during divination sessions to heighten psychic abilities. Hang a sachet of dried berries on a bedpost or place it on a bedside table to end nightmares. Place three berries on your altar to aid in turning inward during the dark of the year to nurture yourself, and then burn them at Yule.

If you have a spirit in your house that troubles you, hang sachets with yew leaves and berries or sprigs of yew in active areas on the dark moon. As you do this, suggest that the spirit follow the energy of the yew to find peace and rest in the otherworld. On the full moon, take the sprigs or sachets down and burn them.

Yew is associated with the elements air, fire, and water. Its astrological influence comes from Jupiter, Mars, and Saturn. This tree is also associated with the following deities: Badb, Banba, Cailleach Bheur, the Dagda, Dôn, Hecate, Hermes, Holle, Loki, Lugh, Odin, and Saturn.

*Figure 40. Yew is associated with the ogham Ioho and the runes Eihwaz, Algiz, and Hagalaz (shown left to right).*

## In the House
### *Focus on Roots*
Roots should be harvested in the autumn or early spring when they are the focus of plant energy, which makes them more potent for medicinal and magical purposes. The roots of annuals can be harvested anytime after the plant is finished blooming or producing seeds. Roots of biennials can be harvested in the autumn of their first year or the following spring. The roots of perennials can be harvested in the autumn or spring. Information for harvesting other parts of plants is covered in "August."

On a day when the soil is moist, not wet, use a shovel, spading fork, or trowel (depending on the size of the plant) to loosen the ground around it. Get the shovel under the roots and gently pry the whole plant from the soil. Trim off stems to within one inch of the root and wipe off any excess soil.

After roots are harvested, wash and scrub them with water, and then cut them into small, one- or two-inch pieces for drying. The cut roots can be kept in the fridge up to forty-eight hours before drying. Small roots that you want to use as amulets can be left whole to dry. Because they are dense, roots take longer to dry than other parts of plants. However, the process can be jump-started by using the oven.

Place a layer of paper towels on a cookie sheet and then spread out the root pieces in a single layer. Set the oven at the lowest temperature for three to four hours. Leave the door ajar to allow air circulation and to keep the roots from baking. Check them every hour and turn them over for uniform drying. Transfer the roots to a screen and place it in a warm room to complete the drying process. Once dry, the roots can be ground into a powder with a food processor.

..................

## ANGELICA

(*Angelica archangelica*)
> *Also known as angelic herb, archangel, common angelica,
> garden angelica, and masterwort

At five to eight feet tall, angelica is best described as statuesque. Its hollow stalks are round and purplish with branching stems. The large, bright green leaflets have coarsely-toothed edges. Tiny honey-scented, white or greenish flowers grow in globe-shaped umbels that bloom mid to late summer of the second or third year. Although angelica is a biennial, it can live for three years. Ribbed on one side, the seeds turn pale brownish yellow when ripe. The yellowish-gray root is long, thick, and fleshy.

In medieval Latin this plant was called *herba angelica*, "angelic herb," because it was believed to be powerful enough to protect against the plague, enchantments, and evil spirits. Angelica was used in spells and rituals and it was worn for protection against spirits and witches. This herb was believed to be especially useful against dark magic. Over time, the use of angelica was adapted from Pagan festivals into Christian celebrations of Saint

Michael. It was a prized medicinal herb for centuries and a valuable commodity during the Renaissance.

First and foremost angelica is a protector, a guardian angel so to speak. Burn pieces of dried root to protect against hexes, to break hexes, and to banish all forms of negativity. Angelica also provides protection during dream work and divination. Hold pieces of root after ritual or magic work to aid in grounding your energy. It also aids in keeping secrets. Smoke from the burning root is ideal for consecrating ritual and magic tools, and altars.

Angelica is associated with the element fire and the goddess Venus. Its astrological influence comes from the sun.

*Figure 41. Angelica is associated with the rune Algiz.*

## CHICORY
(*Cichorium intybus*)
   *Also known as blue sailors, coffeeweed, and succory

Reaching two to three feet tall, and sometimes more, this perennial has a rough, stiff stem and spreading, angular branches. The lower leaves are long, narrow, coarsely toothed, and reminiscent of the dandelion. Sparse leaves on the branches are smaller. Chicory's sky-blue flowers have rayed petals with ragged ends. Blooming from July to November, the flowers grow in clusters of two or three; they open and close at the same time every day. Chicory was introduced from Europe and is now naturalized throughout the United States and southern Canada.

Cultivated in Egypt five thousand years ago, chicory was used medicinally for a variety of ailments throughout the Middle Ages.[113] The root is still used for some remedies and the leaves are used for cooking and in salads. Chicory is best known as an additive to coffee, giving it a slightly bitter taste but said to take the edge off the caffeine. In addition, this familiar roadside weed is a cousin to endive (*Cichorium endivia*), and the vegetable radicchio (*Cichorium intybus* 'Radicchio') is actually a variety of chicory.

---

113   Kowalchik and Hylton, *Rodale's Illustrated Encyclopedia of Herbs*, 85.

Carry a piece of dried root to help remove obstacles and banish turmoil from your life. Carrying it also helps to forget a former lover. Sprinkle dried root on your altar for aid in discerning your particular spiritual path. Use it in spells to unlock opportunities and in magical workings where secrecy is essential. Burning the root with incense aids clarity in divination.

Chicory is associated with the element air. Its astrological influence comes from the sun, Uranus, and the fixed stars Polaris and Vega

## SNAKEROOT
Vermont Snakeroot (*Asarum canadense*)
> *Also known as Canadian wild ginger, colicroot, false coltsfoot, Indian ginger, and wild ginger

Snakeroot forms dense mounds up to a foot tall with glossy, round, five- to six-inch leaves that grow directly from the rhizome. Sometimes, the leaves are more heart-shaped than round. Snakeroot is often grown in the garden as a ground cover plant. Small, fleshy, brownish-purple flowers are bottle-shaped and hidden under the leaves. Blooming from March to June, the flowers are said to give off a terrible odor. Oddly enough, the rhizome is used to make an essential oil.

The common name snakeroot may have come from its European cousin (*Asarum europaeum*), which was used for treating snake bites, or possibly because clumps of young shoots look like a den of little snakes. When cut or crushed, the rhizome smells similar to true ginger (*Zingiber officinale*) and is sometimes used as a substitute for it. Vermont snakeroot should not be confused with Virginian snakeroot (*Aristolochia serpentaria*), which is toxic. Virginian snakeroot has narrow, pointed leaves.

Snakeroot aids in attracting luck, money, and prosperity. Carry a piece of dried root as a talisman or burn it for spell work. Also use it to help maneuver your way into a situation when directness may not work. Burn the root for ritual purification and to build protection especially from hexes. Snakeroot's grounding energy provides stability that augments psychic work. Hold a piece of root to aid in connecting with the otherworld.

Snakeroot is associated with the element earth, and its astrological influence comes from Mars.

November is a good time to walk in the woods or around your neighborhood to look at tree roots. Roots are often only visible between periods of cover from green vegetation and autumn leaves or snow. You may find that roots create beautiful, intricate patterns as they seem to hold the landscape in a comforting hug. Leave offerings on these visible roots in appreciation for a tree's magical energy.

# December

As the wheel of the year makes its final turn and begins a new cycle, many plants have faded or died, but evergreens live up to their name and this is their time of year to shine. With sacred trees, mistletoe, and other plants taken into the home, it is no accident that this is a magical time of year. The name for this month comes from the Latin *decem*, meaning "ten," as it was the tenth month on the Roman calendar.[114]

## On the Calendar

### *December 21/22: Yule/Winter Solstice*

The winter solstice is an event that has been celebrated around the world by civilizations throughout time. As a time of transformation, Yule celebrates the return of the sun/son, which brings hope and the promise of ongoing life. While the Celts had established Samhain as the beginning of the New Year, tenth-century Norse Pagans changed their new year to Yule to coincide with the solar cycle.

---

114   Payack, *A Million Words and Counting*, 176.

Evergreens were considered sacred because they didn't seem to die each year like other trees. Bringing them indoors embodied the reborn spirit of the Green Man. The red of the holly berries represented the blood and fertility of the Goddess, while the white of mistletoe berries symbolized the sacred seed of the God.

Traditionally, the Yule log was a large forest log. Burning it symbolically burned away all vestiges of the old year, and along with it negativity was dispelled. The great log also represented the God of vegetation, which is why Yule log ashes were believed to have special powers of fertility. In nature, fire prepares the way for rebirth.

Representing the light and dark halves of the year, the oak king and holly king trade places at the solstices. Yule marks the succession from the holly (king of the waning year) to the oak (king of the waxing year). Holly represented death, and oak represented rebirth.

### December 24: The Celtic Month of Birch Begins

Birch is associated with new beginnings, protection, purification and the increasing sunlight. It was one of the trees traditionally used for Maypoles

............
### BIRCH

Paper Birch (*Betula papyrifera*)
   *Also known as canoe birch, silver birch, and white birch

Silver Birch (*B. pendula* syn. *B. alba*, *B. verrucosa*)
   *Also known as common birch, European white birch,
    lady of the woods, and warty birch

Paper birch grows fifty to seventy feet tall and can have one or several slender trunks. Its pointed, oval leaves are irregularly toothed and about four inches long. They are dull green on top and lighter underneath, and turn bright yellow in autumn. In the early spring, yellowish-brown male flowers grow in drooping catkins and greenish female flowers grow in smaller, upright catkins. The tree's white bark peels in strips revealing orange-brown inner bark.

The silver birch typically grows thirty to forty feet tall. Its oval, toothed leaves are glossy and have long tapered tips. They turn greenish yellow in the autumn. Silver birch also has yellowish-brown male flowers in drooping catkins and greenish female flowers in smaller, upright catkins that appear in early spring. This tree's bark becomes black and rugged at the base of the tree.

While the genus name *Betula* is the Latin name for the tree, some sources say that it originated from Celtic *betu*, meaning "tree."[115] The species name is from the Greek *papurus*, meaning "papyrus" or "paper," and *fero*, "to bear" or "to carry," making this the paper-bearing tree.[116]

In Wales, birch was associated with love, and in German folklore it was the tree of life. Throughout Europe it was used medicinally. According to legend, Siberian shamans used birch in initiation rituals. Because the wood was often used for broom handles, birch eventually became affiliated with witches. In western England, crosses made of birch twigs were hung over doorways for protection against enchantment.

Use birch twigs to symbolically sweep and clear away negative energy before ritual. Also do this for protection during magic work. Burn a few small pieces of bark for purification and to attract abundance. As a symbol of birth and renewal, birch helps us learn from the past when we want to make a fresh start. For aid in this, place a couple of small twigs on your altar during times of transition.

Hold a twig before a divination session to focus your energy. It will help to bring clarity and aid in receiving knowledge. Use pieces of bark in a sachet for love spells, and place a twig under the bed to aid in fertility. Crumble and sprinkle pieces of bark around your property to attract fairies.

Birch is associated with the element water. In addition to fairies, it is associated with the deities Angus, Cerridwen, the Dagda, Freya, Frigg, Lugh, and Thor. This tree's astrological influence comes from Jupiter, the moon, the sun, and Venus.

*Figure 42. Birch is associated with the ogham Beith and the runes Berkana and Uruz (shown left to right).*

---

115   Small, *North American Cornucopia*, 497.

116   *Ibid.*

# In the Garden
## *Bay*
(*Laurus nobilis*)

> *Also known as bay laurel, bay tree, laurel, Roman laurel, sweet bay, and true laurel

Bay might be more familiar as a small potted tree that is often cut into pom-poms or other topiary shapes. It is an evergreen that can grow up to fifty feet tall, but it is most often kept pruned as a shrub. Growing on short stems, the dark green, leathery leaves are oval and sharply pointed. The small, greenish-yellow flowers grow in inconspicuous clusters and bloom in the early spring. The oval berries are small and turn bluish black when ripe.

Bay is a lovely tree for a garden if you live in the right hardiness zone. Luckily, it grows well in a container so those of us in the north can enjoy it, too. Bay works well as a houseplant because it is a slow grower that takes several years to reach two feet tall. The scent of bay complements the other aromas of the holiday season. Add bay leaves to a door wreath as well as your Yule altar.

It was customary for ancient Greeks and Romans to praise people of accomplishment with crowns of bay. To the Greeks, it was considered a powerful support for divination and prophecy, while to the Romans it symbolized wisdom.

Bay aids in prophetic dreaming, divination, and clairvoyance. Burn a leaf to increase psychic skills. In addition, its purification properties provide protection during this work. Bay also clears and protects the home from negativity. Hang a sprig of bay leaves in the kitchen to invite abundance.

Use dried leaves to enhance defensive magic and remove hexes. Prepare food with bay to aid in personal protection. Carry a leaf to ward off negative energy. At Yule, hold a bay leaf as you visualize your wishes and desires for the coming year, and then throw it on the bonfire or burn it in your cauldron.

Bay is associated with the elements air and fire. Its astrological influence comes from the sun. This tree is also associated with the following deities: Adonis, Apollo, Artemis, Asclepius, Balder, Ceres, Cernunnos, Gaia, Helios, Mars, and Ra.

## Cedar

Atlas Cedar (*Cedrus atlantica*)

    \*Also known as blue Atlas cedar

Red Cedar (*Juniperus virginiana*)

    \*Also known as eastern red cedar and red juniper

In addition to being a type of tree, cedar is a term that refers to conifers (cone-bearing trees) that have fragrant wood. Reaching forty to sixty feet tall, the Atlas cedar is a true cedar that was imported to North America. Young trees have a pyramid shape; older ones become flat-topped. Its one-inch long needles curve toward the tips of branches and range in color from dark green to silvery-blue. The cylindrical cones grow to about three inches long and sit upright on the branches.

The red cedar is not a true cedar, but a type of juniper. Growing thirty to sixty-five feet tall, it has a dense conical shape. Its dark blue, scale-like foliage sometimes turns brownish green in the winter. This tree produces small, yellowish male pollen cones and green female seed cones that develop into blue juniper berries. Like other junipers, it has separate male and female trees. The wood of this tree is popular for cedar chests. In addition, essential oil is extracted from the wood of both of these trees.

The genus name of true cedars, *Cedrus*, comes from the Arabic word *kedron*, meaning "power."[117] In ancient Egypt, cedar oil and incense was used for an offering to the gods. According to Native American folklore, the legendary Thunderbird was believed to nest in a cedar tree high in the mountains.

The scent of cedarwood stimulates dream work and strengthens psychic abilities with focus and clarity. Burning a little wood supports element magic, clairvoyance, and all forms of divination while offering psychic protection. It also aids in communicating with spirits. Use boughs to sweep ritual areas, and keep a few small sprigs with your magic tools for purification.

---

117   Gabriel Mojay, *Aromatherapy for Healing the Spirit: Restoring Emotional and Mental Balance with Essential Oil* (Rochester, VT: Healing Arts Press, 1999), 58.

Use the foliage in spells to attract love or to keep a lover faithful. Burn a little piece of wood for inspiration or when seeking peace of mind. Make a reed diffuser (see the entry in "February" for instructions) with cedarwood oil to foster tranquility in your home.

These trees are associated with all four elements. Their astrological influence comes from Jupiter, Mercury, and the sun. They are associated with the following deities: Arianrhod, Artemis, Astarte, Baal, Brigid, Ea, Odin, Osiris, Persephone, and Ra.

## In the Wild
### Fir
Balsam Fir (*Abies balsamea*)
  *Also known as balsam, blister fir, Canadian balsam, and eastern fir
White Fir (*A. concolor*)
  *Also known as Rocky Mountain white fir

The balsam fir can grow up to eighty feet tall and has a narrow, spire-like crown. Its bark is a grayish color. The branches grow at right angles from the trunk; the lower ones droop. The flat, curved needles are a little over an inch long. They are dark green on top and silvery-blue below. The oblong to cylindrical cones are grayish green with a purple tinge and stand upright on the branches.

The white fir typically grows forty to seventy feet tall, but in the wild it can reach over one hundred feet. It has a narrow, conical shape with a spire-like crown. With age, the crown becomes flattened. The flat, pale blue-green needles are over two inches long and have the same color on both sides. Its barrel-shaped cones are three to six inches long. They are yellowish-green and turn brownish purple with age. They stand upright on the branches.

Throughout Europe, the fir tree was considered the king of the forest and home to powerful woodland spirits. Because it was associated with Artemis/Diana, huntsmen would hang a wolf's head from a fir tree as an offering while asking for her protection. In the past, fir tree resin had a wide range of medicinal uses in Europe and North America.

Fir is a tree of beginnings, energy, growth, and healing. Burn fir needles for purification before ritual and in preparation to receive inspiration. Burn or hold a few needles for grounding energy after ritual or magic work. Holding a sprig of needles or a cone fosters clear communication and creative expression. Place a sprig in your workspace for inspiration.

As an all-purpose purifier, fir provides protection and helps to overcome and remove hexes. The scent of fir heightens awareness for divination and spiritual work, and is especially effective for connecting with forest spirits. Use a sprig of fir or a couple of cones for money and prosperity spells, and for support during channeling.

Fir is associated with the elements air, earth, and fire. Its astrological influence comes from Jupiter, Mars, and Saturn. This tree is associated with Artemis, Athena, Bacchus, Cybele, Diana, Dionysus, Frigg, Inanna, Isis, Osiris, Pan, and Persephone.

*Figure 43. Fir is associated with the ogham Ailm.*

## Mistletoe

American Mistletoe (*Phoradendron leucarpum* syn.
   *Phoradendron flavescens*)
   *Also known as oak mistletoe

Mistletoe is a semiparasitic evergreen shrub with greenish branches that grow in clumps. Although it is sometimes called oak mistletoe, it actually grows in a wide range of trees. Mistletoe clumps are most visible in the winter on deciduous trees. Its thick, leathery leaves are oval to round, and one to two inches long. The inconspicuous flowers are white or greenish-white, and the berries are white or yellowish. This plant is related to the European mistletoe (*Viscum album*).

While its roots tap into the host tree's circulatory system for water and minerals, this species of mistletoe has chlorophyll and produces its own food. It is not generally considered a serious pest. However, the plants that grow in western states called dwarf mistletoe from the genus *Arceuthobium* are parasitic and harmful to their hosts.

There is no end to the stories of how ancient Druids gathered mistletoe. However, Celtic scholar Peter Berresford Ellis believes that Pliny's description of the elaborate procedure may have been mistakenly attributed to Celtic Druids instead of the Germanic tribes on the continent near Gaul.[118] One thing that is certain is that mistletoe was considered powerfully magic, especially for fertility. At Yule, its white berries are plentiful and symbolize the sacred seed of the God, who embodies the spirit of vegetation and the divine spark of life.

In Norse mythology, after the god Balder was slain by a spear made of mistletoe, his mother Frigg was inconsolable. Taking pity on her, the other gods brought Balder back to life. Frigg declared that from that time forward, the mistletoe would be a plant for love, not death. Mistletoe's association with love and fertility remains to this day with our custom of kissing under a sprig of it at Yule. In the past, it was believed that sweethearts who kissed under it were destined to marry, but only if the mistletoe was burned on Twelfth Night.

Make a ring of berries around the base of a green candle for fertility spells. Use mistletoe leaves for spells to attract love and romance. To provide protection, hang a large sprig in an area of your home where it will not be seen often. Allow it to dry and stay in place all year, and then burn it on the following Yule.

Hanging a small sprig in the kitchen attracts blessings. Use it in rituals along with holly for balance of male and female energy. As a plant of in-between places, hold a sprig for astral travel or journeying.

Mistletoe is associated with the element air, and its astrological influence comes from Mercury and the sun. It is associated with the following deities: Apollo, Arianrhod, Asclepius, Balder, Frigg, Jupiter, Odin, Venus, and Zeus.

*Figure 44. Mistletoe is associated with the rune Sowelu.*

---

118    Peter Berresford Ellis, *A Brief History of the Druids* (New York: Carroll & Graf Publishers, 2002), 61.

## *Pine*

Eastern White Pine (*Pinus strobus*)
   *Also known as northern pine, northern white pine, soft pine,
   and white pine

Ponderosa Pine (*P. ponderosa*)
   *Also known as silver pine, western pitch pine, western red pine,
   and western yellow pine

Scots Pine (*P. sylvestris*)
   *Also known as Scotch pine

Eastern white pine typically grows seventy-five to one hundred feet tall. Its smooth, gray bark breaks into small plates as the tree matures. Growing in bundles of five, the dark green needles are three to five inches long, soft and flexible. The cones are four to eight inches long and hang underneath the branches.

Ponderosa pine ranges between one hundred fifty and two hundred feet tall. The scaly, dark-brown bark matures into irregular-shaped, reddish-brown plates. The dark, yellow-green needles grow in bundles of two or three and are five to ten inches long. They are stiff with sharp points. Slender oval cones start out greenish yellow brown but turn glossy and reddish brown. They are six inches long and grow in clusters of three.

Typically growing thirty to sixty feet tall in parks and yards, Scots pine can reach one hundred feet in the wild. It has a conical to columnar shape and distinctive flaking, reddish-brown bark. Growing in pairs, the blue-green needles are about three inches long. The gray or light brown cones are also about three inches long and hang from the branches. Native to Europe, this pine was introduced into North America during Colonial times.

Pine is associated with Pan and other woodland gods, and the species name of the Scots pine, *sylvestris*, means "of the woods or forests."[119] Extensively used for shipbuilding in ancient Greece, pine was dedicated to the sea god Neptune. Various parts of the tree were used medicinally throughout Europe and Asia. To the Romans, pine symbolized the powers of male virility.

---

119   Bill Neal, *Gardener's Latin: Discovering the Origins, Lore & Meanings of Botanical Names* (Chapel Hill, NC: Algonquin Books of Chapel Hill, 1992), 120.

This tree is well known for its purification properties and for dispelling negative energy. It is especially effective in public spaces. The same qualities also make it an ally in defensive magic and for protection from hexes, especially for the home. Burn a few dried needles for these purposes. Use the cones to represent blessings and to attract abundance. Also use them for spells that banish or bind. The scent of pine can steady and focus the mind for psychic work and for communication with spirits. On a spiritual level, pine aids in healing, growth, inspiration, and access to ancient wisdom. Carry a few scales from a pinecone for confidence and courage, especially when dealing with legal matters.

Pine is associated with the elements air, earth, and fire. Its astrological influence comes from Jupiter, Mars, and Saturn. This tree is also associated with the following deities: Aphrodite, Artemis, Astarte, Attis, Bacchus, Cybele, Diana, Dionysus, Ishtar, Isis, Pan, Poseidon, Rhea, Silvanus, Venus, and Vulcan.

*Figure 45. Pine is associated with the oghams Ailm and Ifin, and the rune Kenaz (shown left to right).*

### Spruce

Black Spruce (*Picea mariana*)
  *Also known as bog spruce and swamp spruce

Norway Spruce (*P. abies* syn. *P. excelsa*)
  *Also known as mountain spruce

White Spruce (*P. glauca*)
  *Also known as Black Hills spruce and Canadian spruce

Black spruce is native to North America and usually grows forty-five to sixty feet tall. Its branches are short, and its bark is scaly, grayish brown. Older trees have a spike-like crown. Its stiff, blue-green needles are less than an inch long. The egg-shaped cones are purplish brown, less than two inches long, and grow in clusters.

Native to Europe, Norway spruce has been widely planted in North America. It has a pyramid shape and typically reaches between forty and sixty feet tall, occasionally one hundred feet. Small branches hang from upward-arching main branches. The deep green needles are about an inch long, and the cylindrical cones nine inches.

White spruce is native to North America. It usually grows sixty to eighty feet tall but can reach over one hundred feet. The gray-brown bark is smooth but becomes scaly with age. Its blue-green needles are less than an inch long. The needles have a waxy, white coating, which is the source of this tree's common and species names. When crushed, the needles are pungently aromatic. The pale brown cones are cylindrical and less than three inches long.

The genus name *Picea* was derived from the Latin *pix*, which means "pitch," referring to the tree's resin.[120] Its symmetrical shape has made spruce the quintessential Yule tree in Europe and the United States. In Bavaria, Germany, only spruce and birch were special enough to be used for Maypoles.

Burn spruce needles or pieces of bark to stimulate psychic abilities especially for channeling. Spruce helps develop intuition and to discern when to act on it. Use needles or cones to connect with the energy of forest spirits. Place a sprig on your altar for aid in finding inspiration, deepening spirituality, or strengthening trust. Holding a cone grounds and stabilizes energy after ritual or magic work. Hang a bough anywhere in the home for protection. Also use needles or cones to raise energy in healing circles.

Spruce is associated with the elements earth and water. It is also associated with the following deities: Attis, Cerridwen, Cybele, Danu, and Poseidon.

*Figure 46. Spruce is associated with the rune Dagaz.*

---

120    Fred Hageneder, *The Meaning of Trees: Botany, History, Healing, Love* (San Francisco: Chronicle Books, LLC, 2005), 224.

······································

## Is That a Pine, Fir, or Spruce Tree?

While pine, fir, and spruce trees can be difficult to tell apart, you don't have to be a botanist to figure out which is which. The cones and needles provide clues to help identify them.

| Table 6. Pine, Spruce, and Fir Identification | | | |
|---|---|---|---|
| | Pine | Spruce | Fir |
| Cones | Hang pointing down; Rigid with woody scales | Hang pointing down; Flexible | Stand upright on branch |
| Needles | Grow in clusters | Grow individually; Roll easily between fingers | Grow individually; Flat, not easy to roll between fingers |

## In the House
### Poinsettia
(*Euphorbia pulcherrima* syn. *E. erythrophylla*, *Poinsettia pulcherrima*)
    *Also known as flame leaf

In Mexico, the poinsettia is a shrub that can reach ten to fifteen feet tall. For most of us, these subtropical plants are strictly houseplants. The poinsettia has a woody stem and large, dark-green leaves with slightly wavy edges reminiscent of holly. What we usually think of as big red flower petals are actually modified leaves called bracts that help direct insects to the flowers. The actual flowers are the little yellow clusters in the center of the bracts. Poinsettia stems have a thick, milky sap that can cause skin irritation. However, despite rumors that persisted for years, the plant is not poisonous.

Aztecs cultivated the poinsettia for its brilliant red color, which symbolized purity and the need for sacrifice.[121] In addition to rituals, poinsettias were used medicinally, and during the fifteenth and sixteenth centuries, they were used for trade in the markets of

---

121    J. John, *A Christmas Compendium* (New York: Continuum Books, 2005), 91.

Tenochtitlan, present day Mexico City. According to legend, seventeenth-century friars added the plant to nativity processions beginning this plant's association with Christmas and a range of little drummer boy-like stories.

The plant was named for Joel Poinsett, the American ambassador to Mexico who introduced it into the United States in 1825.[122] The species name, *pulcherrima*, is Latin and means "most beautiful."[123]

Although the poinsettia has had little magical use, its red and green colors fit with the scheme of the season representing ongoing life. It is also appropriate for the Yule altar because the tiny yellow flower and ray of red bracts resemble a brilliant sunburst welcoming the return of the light.

### Pomander Ball/Clove Orange

The pomander ball or clove orange is a traditional winter air freshener that can enhance the atmosphere of our homes and support magic. It is created by pressing the stalks of cloves into an orange. The ball was usually hung in the bedroom to freshen the air and enhance sleep. In addition, it helped to keep moths away from clothing. Once hung, a pomander ball can last for several years, becoming smaller as it dries out. A ripe Seville or other thin-skinned orange works best. The clove orange became a Christmas tradition in Colonial America and has remained popular ever since.

**Making a Pomander Ball:**

1 orange

A couple handfuls of cloves

1 teaspoon orris root, powdered

1 teaspoon cinnamon, ground

1 teaspoon nutmeg, ground

Tissue paper

Ribbon

1 or 2 straight pins

---

122  Barbara J. Euser, ed., *Gardening Among Friends: 65 Practical Essays by Master Gardeners* (Palo Alto, CA: Solas House, 2006), 177.

123  Coombes, *Dictionary of Plant Names*, 139.

To get your pomander ball started, begin pressing cloves into the orange at the top where the stem was attached. It may be easier to start the holes with a skewer and then press the cloves in. The traditional way to make it is to circle the cloves around the orange in one big spiral until the whole fruit is covered. As you work, you may want to chant or recite an incantation to infuse it with magical energy.

When the ball is finished, mix the orris root powder, cinnamon, and nutmeg on a plate, and then roll the orange in the mixture. Other spices can be used, just follow your nose to create a combination that you like. Wrap the orange in tissue paper and store it in a dark place for two weeks.

After two weeks, take the orange out and finish decorating it. Starting at the top of the orange, wrap the ribbon around it. At the bottom of the orange, cross the ribbon at a 90-degree angle and bring the ends back to the top. The ribbon is basically quartering the orange. Secure the ribbon at the bottom of the orange with a straight pin pushed into the orange. You may need a second straight pin to secure the top of the ribbon, too. Tie the ribbon in a bow or make a loop for hanging it.

In addition to scenting the air, a clove orange can be used for magical purposes. Although the orange is usually completely covered with cloves, you may choose to create designs with them.

Create the moon phases on an orange for an esbat celebration or pentagrams for other rituals. Use shapes such as runes, oghams, astrological symbols, or anything that suits your magical purpose.

### Clove
(*Syzygium aromaticum* syn. *Eugenia caryophyllata*)

The familiar clove is actually a dried, unopened flower bud. In addition to being one of the earliest spices used in trade, it also served as an all-purpose medicine. Today cloves are used for medicinal and culinary purposes worldwide.

### Seville Orange
(*Citrus aurantium*)
*Also known as bitter orange and sour orange

It is thought that an orange may have been the so-called golden apple in Greek legend that Gaia presented to Zeus. Oranges have been used as food and medicine for thousands of years. Although we may take them for granted, they were once a highly prized luxury item in cooler climates.

Clove is exceptional at banishing negative energy, and together with the strength of the orange, the pomander ball makes a good amulet for protection. Place one or two in a bowl and set them in an area where you feel a potential threat may come. Oranges are excellent for pre-ritual purification and an aid for divination, dream work, and communication with spirits. The power of cloves amplifies psychic awareness. Because both cloves and oranges help focus the mind and stimulate creativity, hang or place a pomander ball in your workspace. Also, create one to boost the energy of spell work.

Clove is associated with the elements air, earth, and fire. Its astrological influence comes from Jupiter, Mars, Mercury, and the sun. Orange is associated with the elements fire and water. Its astrological influence comes from the sun.

# Summary

From the smallest herb to the tallest tree, magic can be found everywhere in the green world. As we have seen, working with plants in the context of the seasons brings their wisdom alive and boosts the power of our rituals and spells. Following the life cycles of plants month by month for magic work provides continuity and flow to our magic and our everyday lives.

As we have learned, scientific names are crucial in correctly identifying plants. This is important for our own safety in knowing which plants are poisonous or toxic and which are endangered or threatened species. Familiarize yourself with the plants that grow in your area, even in your own neighborhood. Look to your local Native Plant Society for information on walking tours, classes, and books. Over time, a mundane field guide can become almost like a book of shadows as you jot notes in the margins so you can remember where and when you found particular plants.

Basing our magical use of plants within the seasons helps us develop additional and more meaningful ways to connect with the green world and nature spirits. When we invest the time in learning about and working with plants, we may find that they provide us with information on how to employ them in our magic.

Working more closely with plants and the cycle of nature connects us with all the wise women and men who have gone before us. By developing an intimate knowledge of plants, we carry on their magical work and find our unique ways of self-expression in the craft.

# Appendix A:
# Plant List and Quick Guide

The following list will aid you in finding plants and their scientific names quickly. Included is the month (or months) in which you can find their details.

**Aconite** [August]
> Common Monkshood (*Aconitum napellus*)
> Wolfsbane (*A. lycoctonum*)

**Adder's Tongue** [March]
> Northern Adder's Tongue (*Ophioglossum pusillum*)
> American Trout-lily (*Erythronium americanum*)

**African Violet** (*Saintpaulia ionantha*) [January]

**Agrimony** [August]
> Common Agrimony (*Agrimonia eupatoria*)

**Alder** [March]
  Common Alder (*Alnus glutinosa*)

**Aloe** (*Aloe vera*) [January]

**Amaryllis** (*Hippeastrum* spp.) [January, February]

**Angelica** (*Angelica archangelica*) [January, November]

**Apple** [September]
  Modern Cultivated Apple (*Malus domestica* syn. *Malus pumila, Pyrus pumila*)

**Arnica** (*Arnica montana*) [August]

**Ash** [February]
  Common Ash (*Fraxinus excelsior*)
  White Ash (*F. americana*)

**Bamboo** (*Dracaena sanderiana*) [January]

**Basil** (*Ocimum basilicum*) [August]

**Bay Laurel** (*Laurus nobilis*) [December]

**Beech** [September]
  American Beech (*Fagus grandifolia*)
  Common Beech (*F. sylvatica*)

**Belladonna** (*Atropa belladonna*) [June]

**Belladonna Lily** (*Amaryllis belladonna* syn. *Callicore rosea*) [October]

**Birch** [December]
  Paper Birch (*Betula papyrifera*)
  Silver Birch (*Betula pendula* syn. *B. alba, B. verrucosa*)

**Bistort** [September]
  Common Bistort (*Persicaria bistorta* syn. *Polygonum bistorta*)
  Western Bistort (*Persicaria bistortoides* syn. *Polygonum bistortoides*)

**Bittersweet** [October]
American Bittersweet (*Celastrus scandens*)
European Bittersweet (*Solanum dulcamara*)

**Black Hellebore** (*Helleborus niger*) [February]

**Blackberry** [September]
American Blackberry (*Rubus villosus*)
European Blackberry (*R. fruticosus*)

**Blackthorn** (*Prunus spinosa*) [May, October, November]

**Bloodroot** (*Sanguinaria canadensis*) [March]

**Bluebell** [March]
Virginia Bluebell (*Mertensia virginica*)

**Borage** (*Borago officinalis*) [August]

**Burdock** [October]
Greater Burdock (*Arctium lappa*)

**Buttercup** [April]
Creeping Buttercup (*Ranunculus repens*)
Meadow Buttercup (*R. acris*)

**Cactus** [January]
Barrel Cactus (*Echinocactus grusonii*)
Bunny Ears Cactus (*Opuntia microdasys*)

**Catnip** (*Nepeta cataria*) [August]

**Cattails** (*Typha latifolia*) [October]

**Cedar** [December]
Atlas Cedar (*Cedrus atlantica*)
Red Cedar (*Juniperus virginiana*)

**Chamomile** [August]
   Roman Chamomile (*Chamaemelum nobile* syn. *Anthemis nobilis*)
   German Chamomile (*Matricaria recutita*, syn. *M. chamomilla*)

**Cherry** [April, July]
   Black Cherry (*Prunus serotina*)
   Sweet Cherry (*P. avium*)

**Chickweed** [November]
   Common Chickweed (*Stellaria media*)

**Chicory** (*Cichorium intybus*) [November]

**Chrysanthemum** [October]
   Common Chrysanthemum (*Chrysanthemum morifolium* syn. *Dendranthema grandiflorum*, *Anthemis grandiflora*)

**Cinquefoil** [May]
   Creeping Cinquefoil (*Potentilla reptans*)
   Dwarf Cinquefoil (*P. canadensis*)

**Clove** (*Syzygium aromaticum* syn. *Eugenia caryophyllata*) [December]

**Clover** [March]
   White Clover (*Trifolium repens*)

**Coltsfoot** (*Tussilago farfara*) [February]

**Columbine** [May]
   Wild Columbine (*Aquilegia canadensis*)
   Garden Columbine (*A. vulgaris*)

**Comfrey** [May]
   Common Comfrey (*Symphytum officinale*)

**Crabapple** [April]
   American Crabapple (*Malus coronaria* syn. *Pyrus coronaria*)

**Crocus** [February]
    Dutch Crocus (*C. vernus*)
    Early Crocus (*Crocus tommasinianus*)
    Snow Crocus (*C. chrysanthus*)

**Cyclamen** (*Cyclamen persicum*) [January]

**Cypress** [February]
    Italian Cypress (*Cupressus sempervirens*)

**Daffodil** (*Narcissus pseudonarcissus*) [March]

**Daisy** [April]
    Common Daisy (*Bellis perennis*)
    Ox-eye Daisy (*Leucanthemum vulgare* syn. *Chrysanthemum leucanthemum*)

**Dandelion** (*Taraxacum officinale*) [March]

**Datura** (*Datura stramonium*) [July]

**Dill** (*Anethum graveolens* syn. *Peucedanum graveolens*) [July]

**Dogwood** (*Cornus florida*) [March]

**Elder** [June, September, November]
    Common Elder (*Sambucus canadensis*)
    Black Elder (*S. nigra*)

**Elecampane** (*Inula helenium*) [July]

**Eucalyptus** [January]
    Blue Gum Eucalyptus (*Eucalyptus globulus*)

**Evening Primrose** (*Oenothera biennis*) [October]

**Fern** [January]
    Boston Fern (*Nephrolepis exaltata*)
    Maidenhair Fern (*Adiantum raddianum*)

**Fir** [December]
    Balsam Fir (*Abies balsamea*)
    White Fir (*A. concolor*)

**Forsythia** (*Forsythia × intermedia*) [March]

**Foxglove** [June]
    Common Foxglove (*Digitalis purpurea*)

**Geranium** [January]
    Common Geranium (*Pelargonium × hortorum* syn. *P. inquinans*)

**Goldenrod** [September]
    European Goldenrod (*Solidago virgaurea*)
    Sweet Goldenrod (*S. odora*)

**Goosefoot** (*Syngonium podophyllum*) [January]

**Gorse** [November]
    Common gorse (*Ulex europaeus*)

**Gravel Root/Joe Pye Weed** [September]
    Sweet Joe-Pye Weed (*Eutrochium purpureum*)

**Hawthorn** [May, June, October]
    Common Hawthorn (*Crataegus monogyna*)
    English Hawthorn (*C. laevigata* syn. *C. oxyacantha*)

**Hazel** [August, September]
    Common Hazel (*Corylus avellana*)
    American Hazelnut (*C. americana*)

**Heath and Heather** [November]
    Common Heather (*Calluna vulgaris*)
    Hybrid Heath (*Erica × darleyensis*)
    Winter Heath (*E. carnea* syn. *E. herbacea*)

**Henbane** (*Hyoscyamus niger*) [July]

**Holly** [January, July, December]
  American Holly (*Ilex opaca*)
  English Holly (*I. aquifolium*)

**Honeysuckle** [August]
  Common Honeysuckle (*Lonicera periclymenum*)
  Italian Honeysuckle (*L. caprifolium*)

**Hyssop** (*Hyssopus officinalis*) [July]

**Iris** [April]
  Blue Flag Iris (*Iris versicolor*)
  Common Flag Iris (*I. germanica*)
  Florentine Iris (*I. florentina*)
  Sweet Flag Iris (*I. pallida*)

**Ivy** [September]
  Common Ivy (*Hedera helix*)

**Jasmine** [November]
  Winter Jasmine (*Jasminum nudiflorum*)

**Juniper** [November]
  Common Juniper (*Juniperus communis*)

**Lady's Mantle** [June]
  Common Lady's Mantle (*Alchemilla vulgaris*)
  Soft Lady's Mantle (*A. mollis*)

**Lavender** [July]
  English Lavender (*Lavandula angustifolia*, syn. *L. officinalis*)

**Lilac** [May]
  Common Lilac (*Syringa vulgaris*)

**Lily of the Valley** (*Convallaria majalis*) [May]

**Locust** [October]
  Honey Locust (*Gleditsia triacanthos*)
  Black Locust (*Robinia pseudoacacia*)

**Maple** [September]
  Sugar Maple (*Acer saccharum*)

**Marigold** [October]
  African Marigold (*Tagetes erecta* syn. *T. major*)
  French Marigold (*T. patula*)

**Masterwort** (*Imperatoria ostruthium* syn. *Peucedanum ostruthium*) [January]

**Meadowsweet** (*Filipendula ulmaria* syn. *Spiraea ulmaria*) [June]

**Mint** [June]
  Peppermint (*Mentha × piperita*)
  Spearmint (*M. spicata*, syn. *M. viridis*)

**Mistletoe** [December]
  American Mistletoe (*Phoradendron leucarpum* syn. *Phoradendron flavescens*)

**Moon Flower** (*I. alba* syn. *I. bona-nox, Calonyction aculeatum*) [July]

**Morning Glory** [July]
  Common Morning Glory (*Ipomoea purpurea* syn. *Convolvulus purpureus, Pharbitis purpurea*)

**Mugwort** (*Artemisia vulgaris*) [July]

**Mullein** [June]
  Common Mullein (*Verbascum thapsus*)
  Dark Mullein (*V. nigrum*)

**Oak** [June, September]
  Black Oak (*Quercus velutina*)
  White Oak (*Q. alba*)

**Orange** [December]
  Seville Orange (*Citrus aurantium*)

**Pansy** [March]
    Garden Pansy (*Viola × wittrockiana*)
    Wild Pansy (*V. tricolor*)

**Pine** [December]
    Eastern White Pine (*Pinus strobus*)
    Ponderosa Pine (*P. ponderosa*)
    Scots Pine (*P. sylvestris*)

**Plantain** [April]
    Broadleaf Plantain (*Plantago major*)
    Buckhorn Plantain (*P. lanceolata*)

**Poinsettia** (*Euphorbia pulcherrima* syn. *E. erythrophylla, Poinsettia pulcherrima*)
    [December]

**Primrose** [April]
    Common Primrose (*Primula vulgaris* syn. *P. acaulis*)
    Polyanthus Primrose (*P. × polyantha*)

**Pumpkin** [October]
    Field Pumpkin (*Cucurbita pepo* var. *pepo*)

**Queen Anne's Lace** (*Daucus carota*) [October]

**Reed** [October]
    Common Reed (*Phragmites australis* syn. *Phragmites communis*)

**Rose** [February, July, September]
    Dog Rose (*Rosa canina*)
    Garden Roses (*Rosa spp.*)

**Rosemary** (*Rosmarinus officinalis*) [May]

**Rowan** [January]
    American Mountain Ash (*Sorbus americana*)
    European Mountain Ash (*S. aucuparia*)

**Sage** [July]

    Common Sage (*Salvia officinalis*)

**Saint John's Wort** (*Hypericum perforatum*) [June]

**Snakeroot** [November]

    Vermont Snakeroot (*Asarum canadense*)

**Snowdrop** (*Galanthus nivalis*) [February]

**Solomon's Seal** (*Polygonatum biflorum*) [April]

**Spider Plant** (*Chlorophytum comosum*) [January]

**Spruce** [December]

    Black Spruce (*Picea mariana*)
    Norway Spruce (*P. abies* syn. *P. excelsa*)
    White Spruce (*P. glauca*)

**Strawberry** [June]

    Garden Strawberry (*Fragaria* × *ananassa*)
    Wild Strawberry (*F. vesca*)

**Sunflower** [August]

    Common Sunflower (*Helianthus annuus*)

**Sweet Woodruff** (*Galium odoratum* syn. *Asperula odorata*) [April]

**Tansy** [September]

    Common Tansy (*Tanacetum vulgare* syn. *Chrysanthemum vulgare*)

**Thyme** (*Thymus vulgaris*) [January]

**Tulip** [April]

    Garden Tulip (*Tulipa gesneriana*)

**Valerian** [May]

    Common Valerian (*Valeriana officinalis*)

**Vervain** (*Verbena officinalis*) [June]

**Violet** [March]
    Common Blue Violet (*Viola sororia* syn. *V. papilionacea*)
    Sweet Violet (*V. odorata*)

**Willow** [April]
    American Willow (*Salix discolor*)
    Weeping Willow (S. *babylonica*)

**Witch Hazel** (*Hamamelis* × *intermedia*) [January]

**Wolfberry** [February]
    Fremont's Wolfberry (*Lycium fremontii*)

**Yarrow** [May]
    Common Yarrow (*Achillea millefolium*)

**Yew** [November]
    American Yew (*Taxus canadensis*)
    English Yew (*T. baccata*)
    Western Yew (*T. brevifolia*)

**Yucca** [March]
    Mojave Yucca (*Yucca Schidigera*)
    Adam's Needle (*Y. filamentosa*)

# Appendix B:
# Magical Correspondences

This listing provides a quick reference to help you find plants to suit your purposes and contains the correspondences covered in this book.

**Abundance:** Acorn, apple, African violet, bay, beechnut, birch, buttercup, cherry, clover, comfrey, crabapple, dill, jasmine, juniper, marigold, oak, pine, Saint John's wort, spider plant, tulip, vervain
Ancestors: Beechnut, cattail, cypress, reed

**Banish:** Alder, angelica, bittersweet, black hellebore, burdock, chicory, clove, comfrey, crocus, cypress, evening primrose, fern, hazel, lilac, mullein, pine, rose, rosehip, vervain, yarrow, yew

**Bind:** Bloodroot (release), comfrey, cypress, ivy, jasmine, locust, moon flower, morning glory, pine, rose, rosemary, Solomon's seal

**Changes/Transformation:** Belladonna lily, birch, borage, evening primrose, goosefoot, hazel, violet

**Communication:** Cedar, chamomile, eucalyptus, fir, hazel, jasmine, orange, pine, rose

**Concentration/Focus:** Clove, eucalyptus, geranium, lady's mantle, lavender, orange, Solomon's seal

**Consecration:** Angelica, chamomile, cypress, eucalyptus, hawthorn, hyssop, lavender, mugwort, rose, sage, sweet woodruff, thyme, valerian, vervain, yarrow

**Courage:** Adder's tongue, angelica, bloodroot, columbine, masterwort, pine, snowdrop

**Creativity:** Ash, beechnut, clove, dill, fir, geranium, hazel, iris, jasmine, lilac, maple, orange

**Death/Funeral Practices:** Apple, belladonna, bittersweet, chrysanthemum, cypress, daffodil, elderflower, henbane, holly, marigold, monkshood, tansy, wolfsbane, yew

**Defense:** Bay, burdock, cypress, dill, elder, goosefoot, gorse, haws, hazel, holly, jasmine, juniper, lilac, mugwort, pine, tansy, wolfberry

**Divination:** Adder's tongue, alder, angelica, apple, arnica, ash, basil, bay, birch, bistort, bloodroot, borage, buttercup, cedar, chamomile, cherry, chicory, crocus, cypress, daisy, dill, dog rose, elecampane, fir, goldenrod, hazel, holly, jasmine, juniper, lady's mantle, lavender, lilac, marigold, mugwort, orange, pansy, peppermint, pumpkin, rose, rosehip, rowan, sage, strawberry, thyme, willow, yarrow, yew

**Dream Work:** Adder's tongue, alder, angelica, ash, bay, catnip, chamomile, coltsfoot, daisy, dog rose, elderberry, eucalyptus, heath or heather, holly, honeysuckle, jasmine, juniper, lavender, lilac, maple, marigold, orange, peppermint, primrose, Queen Anne's lace, rose, rosehip, sunflower, sweet woodruff, thyme, tulip, vervain, violet, wolfberry, yarrow

**Fairies:** Acorn, alder, birch, blackberry, bluebell, crabapple, daisy, dog rose, elder, fern, foxglove, haws, hawthorn, lilac, lily of the valley, primrose, rose, rosemary, thyme, violet, willow

**Fear (dispel):** Clover, jasmine, plantain, snowdrop

**Fertility:** Amaryllis, apple, birch, cherry, chickweed, cyclamen, fern, forsythia, haws, hyssop, mistletoe, oak, Queen Anne's lace, Saint John's wort, spider plant, willow

**Friendship:** Daffodil, lily of the valley, rose, strawberry, wolfberry

**Growth:** Cypress, fir, geranium, pine

**Happiness:** Borage, lily of the valley, marigold, rose, snowdrop, violet

**Healing:** Adder's tongue, aloe, chamomile, cypress, elderberry, evening primrose, fir, heath or heather, hyssop, iris, lady's mantle, lavender, meadowsweet, oak, pine, rose, rosehip, rosemary, sage, spruce, thyme, valerian

**Hexes (remove, ward off):** Agrimony, Angelica, basil, bay, bittersweet, chamomile, cinquefoil, clover, dill, elder, fern, fir, geranium, gorse, hyssop, juniper, lilac, mullein, pine, rose, rosehip, rosemary, snakeroot, valerian, yarrow, yucca

**The Home:** Acorn, African violet, agrimony, basil, bay, cedar, chickweed, chrysanthemum, coltsfoot, comfrey, crocus, daffodil, evening primrose, iris, marigold, meadowsweet, mistletoe, mugwort, pine, pumpkin, reed, rose, spearmint, spider plant, valerian

**Hope:** Snowdrop, violet

**Inspiration:** Ash, cedar, dogwood, fir, hazel, jasmine, pine, spruce

**Jealousy (quell, remove):** Columbine

**Justice/Legal Matters:** Cypress, marigold, pine,

**Loss (recover from):** Chrysanthemum, cypress, hazel

**Love:** African violet, apple, ash, basil, belladonna lily, birch, bloodroot, cedar, chamomile, cherry, chickweed, chrysanthemum, clover, columbine, crabapple, crocus, cyclamen, daffodil, daisy, dandelion, dill, elderberry, elecampane, hawthorn, heath or heather, honeysuckle, iris, jasmine, juniper, lady's mantle, lavender, lilac, maple, meadowsweet, mistletoe, mullein, pansy, peppermint, primrose, Queen Anne's lace, Saint John's wort, strawberry, thyme, tulip, valerian, willow

**Loyalty/Fidelity:** Basil, chickweed, daisy, dogwood, elderberry, honeysuckle, lavender, reed, rosemary, wolfberry

**Luck:** Aloe, bamboo, basil, blackberry, bluebell, chamomile, cherry, daffodil, daisy, dandelion, dill, gravel root, heath or heather, holly, honeysuckle, ivy, jasmine, peppermint, rose, rosehip, snakeroot, strawberry, thyme, tulip

**Manifest (desires, dreams, will):** Acorn, bay, beechnut, bluebell, borage, buttercup, dandelion, dogwood, jasmine, sage, sunflower, violet

**Money/Prosperity:** Apple, basil, beechnut, blackberry, chamomile, crabapple, dill, fir, geranium, goldenrod, haws, juniper, maple, peppermint, pumpkin, sage, snakeroot, spearmint, spider plant, sunflower, thyme, valerian

**Negativity (remove, ward off):** Agrimony, angelica, bamboo, basil, bay, birch, bistort, blackthorn, burdock, chickweed, clove, cyclamen, daffodil, eucalyptus, fern, gravel root, haws, hawthorn, hyssop, ivy, juniper, lavender, lilac, locust, masterwort, mugwort, mullein, oak, pine, plantain, rosemary, sage, Saint John's wort, Solomon's seal, sunflower, sweet woodruff, tansy, thyme, vervain, yarrow, yucca

**Obstacles (remove):** Bluebell, cherry, chicory, locust

**Passion:** Apple, cattail, cyclamen, honeysuckle,

**Peace:** Arnica, bamboo, cedar, coltsfoot, crocus, jasmine, rose

**Protection:** Acorn, agrimony, alder, aloe, angelica, arnica, ash, bay, black hellebore, blackberry, blackthorn, burdock, cactus, cattail, cedar, chrysanthemum, cinquefoil, clove, coltsfoot, comfrey, crabapple, cyclamen, cypress, daffodil, daisy, dogwood, elecampane, eucalyptus, evening primrose, fir, geranium, goosefoot, gorse, hawthorn, hazel, heath or heather, holly, hyssop, iris, juniper, lavender, locust, masterwort, monkshood, mugwort, mullein, orange, reed, rosehip, rosemary, rowan, Saint John's wort, sloes, Solomon's seal, spruce, valerian, willow, wolfberry, wolfsbane, yucca

**Psychic Abilities:** Arnica, basil, bay, bistort, borage, catnip, cedar, chamomile, clove, clover, coltsfoot, comfrey, elecampane, eucalyptus, fir, geranium, hazel, heath or heather, honeysuckle, jasmine, juniper, lavender, marigold, pine, rose, rosehip, rosemary, rowan, sage, spruce, thyme, yarrow, yew

**Purification:** Agrimony, angelica, bay, belladonna lily, birch, bistort, burdock, chamomile, dill, elder, eucalyptus, fir, gorse, hawthorn, hyssop, iris, juniper, masterwort, mugwort, pine, Queen Anne's lace, rosemary, sage, Saint John's wort, snakeroot, spearmint, sweet woodruff, thyme, valerian, yarrow

**Renewal:** Belladonna lily, birch, cypress, daffodil

**Sex/Sexuality:** Adder's tongue, cattail, hyssop, strawberry

**Spirit Guides:** Alder, gravel root, heath or heather, lavender, rowan, sage

**Spirituality:** Adder's tongue, buttercup, chicory, heath or heather, holly, hyssop, lavender, spearmint, spruce

**Strength:** Adder's tongue, angelica, bloodroot, cinquefoil, cypress, hazel, masterwort, oak, snowdrop, sunflower

**Success:** Apple, geranium, gravel root, iris, lily of the valley, marigold, moon flower, morning glory, rowan

**Wisdom:** Acorn, aloe, apple, beechnut, buttercup, crabapple, cypress, elder, hazel, mullein, pine, Solomon's seal

# Bibliography

Albert, Susan Wittig. *China Bayles' Book of Days: 365 Celebrations of the Mystery, Myth, and Magic of Herbs from the World of Pecan Springs*. New York: Penguin Group USA Inc., 2006.

Allen, Linda. *Decking the Halls: The Folklore and Traditions of Christmas Plants*. Minocqua, WI: Willow Creek Press, 2000.

Altman, Nathaniel. *Sacred Trees: Spirituality, Wisdom & Well-Being*. New York: Sterling Publishing Company, Inc., 2000.

Arrowsmith, Nancy. *Essential Herbal Wisdom: A Complete Exploration of 50 Remarkable Herbs*. Woodbury, MN: Llewellyn Worldwide, 2009.

Balick, Michael. *Rodale's 21st Century Herbal: A Practical Guide for Healthy Living Using Nature's Most Powerful Plants*. Emmaus, PA: Rodale Press, Inc., 2014.

Bane, Theresa. *Encyclopedia of Fairies in World Folklore and Mythology*. Jefferson, NC: McFarland & Company, Inc., 2013.

Barceloux, Donald G. *Medical Toxicology of Natural Substances: Foods, Fungi, Medicinal Herbs, Plants, and Venomous Animals*. Hoboken, NJ: John Wiley & Sons, Inc., 2008.

Beyerl, Paul. *A Compendium of Herbal Magic*. Custer, WA: Phoenix Publishing, Inc., 1998.

Blackburne-Maze, Peter. *Fruit: An Illustrated History*. London: Firefly Books, Ltd., 2003.

Blum, Ralph. *The Book of Runes*. London: Headline Book Publishing, 1996.

Bonar, Ann. *Herbs: A Complete Guide to the Cultivation and Use of Wild and Domesticated Herbs*. New York: MacMillan Publishing Co., 1985.

Bradley, Fern Marshall, Barbara W. Ellis, and Ellen Phillips, eds. *Rodale's Ultimate Encyclopedia of Organic Gardening: The Indispensable Resource for Every Gardener*. Emmaus, PA: Rodale Press, Inc., 1977.

Brodie, Janet Farrell. *Contraception and Abortion in Nineteenth-Century America*. Ithaca, NY: Cornell University Press, 1994.

Carr-Gomm, Philip, and Stephanie Carr-Gomm. *The Druid Plant Oracle: Working with the Magical Flora of the Druid Tradition*. London: Eddison Sadd Editions, Limited, 2007.

Charles, Denys J. *Antioxidant Properties of Spices, Herbs and Other Sources*. New York: Springer Science + Business Media, 2013.

Chevallier, Andrew. *The Encyclopedia of Medicinal Plants: A Practical Reference Guide to Over 550 Key Herbs and Their Medicinal Uses*. New York: Dorling Kindersley Publishing, 1996.

Church, Glyn. *Trees and Shrubs for Fragrance*. Buffalo, NY: Firefly Books U.S. Inc., 2002.

Clarkson, Janet. *Food History Almanac: Over 1,300 Years of World Culinary History, Culture and Social Influence, Volume 1*. Lanham, MD: Rowman & Littlefield, 2014.

Coombes, Allen J. *Dictionary of Plant Names*. Portland, OR: Timber Press, Inc., 1985.

Cruden, Loren. *Medicine Grove: A Shamanic Herbal*. Rochester, VT: Destiny Books, 1997.

Cumo, Christopher, ed. *Encyclopedia of Cultivated Plants: From Acacia to Zinnia*. Santa Barbara, CA: ABC-CLIO, 2013.

Cunningham, Scott. *Cunningham's Encyclopedia of Magical Herbs*. St. Paul, MN: Llewellyn Publications, 1998.

Dirr, Michael A. *Dirr's Encyclopedia of Trees and Shrubs*. Portland, OR: Timber Press, Inc., 2011.

Dobelis, Inge N., ed. *Magic and Medicine of Plants: A Practical Guide to the Science, History, Folklore, and Everyday Uses of Medicinal Plants*. Pleasantville, NY: The Reader's Digest Association, Inc., 1986.

Dugan, Ellen. *Garden Witch's Herbal: Green Magick, Herbalism & Spirituality*. Woodbury, MN: Llewellyn Publications, 2014.

Durkin, Philip. *The Oxford Guide to Etymology*. New York: Oxford University Press, 2009.

Dutton, Joan Parry. *Plants of Colonial Williamsburg: How to Identify 200 of Colonial America's Flowers, Herbs, and Trees*. Williamsburg, VA: The Colonial Williamsburg Foundation, 1994.

Edworthy, Niall. *The Curious World of Christmas: Celebrating All That Is Weird, Wonderful, and Festive*. New York: Perigee Books, 2007.

Ellis, Peter Berresford. *A Brief History of the Druids*. New York: Carroll & Graf Publishers, 2002.

Euser, Barbara J., ed. *Bay Area Gardening: 64 Practical Essays by Master Gardeners*. Palo Alto, CA: Solas House, 2005.

———, ed. *Gardening Among Friends: 65 Practical Essays by Master Gardeners*. Palo Alto, CA: Solas House, 2006.

Ferguson, Diane. *The Magickal Year: A Pagan Perspective on the Natural World*. New York: Labyrinth Books, 1996.

Fernie, W. T. *Herbal Simples Approved for Modern Uses of Cure, Second Edition*. Philadelphia: Boericke and Tafel, 1897.

Foster, Steven, and Rebecca L. Johnson. *National Geographic Desk Reference to Nature's Medicine*. Washington, DC: National Geographic Society, 2008.

Freeman, Margaret Beam. *The Unicorn Tapestries*. New York: Metropolitan Museum of Art, 1983.

Fries, Jan. *Cauldron of the Gods: A Manual for Celtic Magic*. Oxford: Mandrake of Oxford, 2003.

Gamache, Henri. *The Magic of Herbs*. Pomeroy, WA: Health Research Books, 2010.

Giesecke, Annette. *The Mythology of Plants: Botanical Lore from Ancient Greece and Rome*. Los Angeles: Getty Publications, 2014.

Gladstar, Rosemary. *Medicinal Herbs: A Beginner's Guide*. North Adams, MA: Storey Publishing, 2012.

———, and Pamela Hirsch, eds. *Planting the Future: Saving Our Medicinal Herbs*. Rochester, VT: Healing Arts Press, 2000.

Gordon, Lesley. *Green Magic: Flowers, Plants, and Herbs in Legend and Lore*. New York: The Viking Press, 1977.

Greer, John Michael. *Encyclopedia of Natural Magic*. Woodbury, MN: Llewellyn Publications, 2005.

Gregg, Susan. *The Complete Illustrated Encyclopedia of Magical Plants, Revised: A Practical Guide to Creating Healing, Protection, and Prosperity using Plants, Herbs, and Flowers*. Beverly, MA: Fair Winds, 2014.

Grieve, Margaret. *A Modern Herbal Volumes 1 and 2*. Mineola, NY: Dover Publications, 1971.

Guyett, Carole. *Sacred Plant Initiations: Communicating with Plants for Healing and Higher Consciousness*. Rochester, VT: Bear & Company, 2015.

Hageneder, Fred. *The Meaning of Trees: Botany, History, Healing, Lore.* San Francisco: Chronicle Books, LLC, 2005.

Hallowell, Barbara G. *Mountain Year: A Southern Appalachian Nature Notebook.* Winston-Salem, NC: John F. Blair, Publisher, 1998.

Harrison, Lorraine. *Latin for Gardeners: Over 3,000 Plant Names Explained and Explored.* Chicago: University of Chicago Press, 2012.

Heilmeyer, Marina. *Ancient Herbs.* Los Angeles: Getty Publications, 2007.

Hessayon, D. G. *The House Plant Expert.* Waltham Cross, England: PBI Publications, 1980.

———. *The Tree & Shrub Expert.* Waltham Cross, England: PBI Publications, 1983.

———. *The Flower Expert.* Waltham Cross, England: PBI Publications, 1984.

Hinton, Sam. *Seashore Life of Southern California, New and Revised Edition.* Berkeley, CA: University of California Press, 1987.

Hogg, Robert, ed. *The Journal of Horticulture, Cottage Gardener, and Home Farmer, Volume VI: Third Series January to July 1883.* London: The Journal of Horticulture, 1883.

Impelluso, Lucia. *Nature and Its Symbols.* Translated by Stephen Sartarelli. Los Angeles: Getty Publications, 2004.

Ivanits, Linda J., *Russian Folk Belief.* New York: Routledge, 2015.

John, J. *A Christmas Compendium.* New York: Continuum Books, 2005.

Jones, Julia, and Barbara Deer. *Cattern Cakes and Lace: A Calendar of Feasts.* London: Dorling Kindersley Ltd., 1987.

———. *The Country Diary of Garden Lore.* London: Dorling Kindersley Ltd., 1989.

Kambos, James. "Enchanting Primroses," *Llewellyn's 2014 Herbal Almanac: Herbs for Growing & Gathering, Cooking & Crafts, Health & Beauty, History, Myth & Lore.* Woodbury, MN: Llewellyn Publications, 2013.

Kear, Katherine. *Flower Wisdom: The Definitive Guidebook to the Myth, Folklore, and Healing Powers of Flowers.* London: Thorsons, 2000.

Khare, C. P., ed. *Indian Herbal Remedies: Rational Western Therapy, Ayurvedic and Other Traditional Usage*. New York: Springer-Verlag, 2004.

Kipfer, Barbara Ann. *The Culinarian: A Kitchen Desk Reference*. Hoboken, NJ: John Wiley & Sons, Inc., 2011.

Kowalchik, Claire, and William H. Hylton, eds. *Rodale's Illustrated Encyclopedia of Herbs*. Emmaus, PA: Rodale Press, Inc., 1998.

Lawless, Julia. *The Illustrated Encyclopedia of Essential Oils: The Complete Guide to the Use of Oils in Aromatherapy and Herbalism*. Rockport, MA: Element Books, Inc., 1995.

MacCoitir, Niall. *Irish Trees: Myths, Legends & Folklore*. Cork, Ireland: The Collins Press, 2003.

MacKillop, James. *Oxford Dictionary of Celtic Mythology*. Oxford: Oxford University Press, 2000.

Martimort, A. G., I. H. Dalmais, and P. Jounel, eds. *The Liturgy and Time: The Church at Prayer: An Introduction to the Liturgy, Volume IV*. Collegeville, MN: Liturgical Press, 1986.

Martin, Laura C. *Wildflower Folklore*. New York: The East Woods Press, 1984.

Masters, Maxwell T. *Vegetable Teratology: An Account of the Principal Deviations from the Usual Construction of Plants*. London: Robert Hardwicke, 1869.

Matthews, Caitlin, and John Matthews. *Encyclopedia of Celtic Wisdom: A Celtic Shaman's Sourcebook*. Rockport, MA: Element Books, 1994.

McCabe, Ina Baghdiantz. *A History of Global Consumption: 1500-1800*. New York: Routledge, 2015.

Medina, Barbara, and Victor Medina. *Central Appalachian Wildflowers*. Guilford, CT: The Globe Pequot Press, 2002.

Metzner, Ralph. *The Well of Remembrance: Rediscovering the Earth Wisdom Myths of Northern Europe*. Boston: Shambhala Publications, Inc., 1994.

Miller, Richard Alan, and Iona Miller. *The Magical and Ritual Use of Perfumes*. Rochester, VT: Destiny Books, 1990.

Mojay, Gabriel. *Aromatherapy for Healing the Spirit: Restoring Emotional and Mental Balance with Essential Oil*. Rochester, VT: Healing Arts Press, 1999.

Molinari, Mario. *Divided by Words: Making a Case for a New Literacy*. Bury St. Edmonds, England: Arena Books, 2009.

Myers, Luke A. *Gnostic Visions: Uncovering the Greatest Secret of the Ancient World*. Bloomington, IN: iUniverse, Inc., 2011.

Neal, Bill. *Gardener's Latin: Discovering the Origins, Lore & Meanings of Botanical Names*. Chapel Hill, NC: Algonquin Books of Chapel Hill, 1992.

Nelson, Gil. *Atlantic Coastal Plain Wildflowers*. Guilford, CT: The Globe Pequot Press, 2006.

Patterson, Rachel. *A Kitchen Witch's World of Magical Herbs & Plants*. Alresford, England: Moon Books, 2014.

Pauwels, Ivo, and Gerty Christoffels. *Herbs: Healthy Living with Herbs from Your Own Garden*. Translated by Milton Webber. Antwerp, The Netherlands: Struik Publishers, 2006.

Payack, Paul J. J. *A Million Words and Counting: How Global English is Rewriting the World*. New York: Citadel Press Books, 2008.

Pennick, Nigel. *Magical Alphabets*. Boston: Red Wheel/Weiser, LLC, 1992.

Pickles, Sheila. *The Language of Flowers*. London: Pavilion Books Limited, 1990.

Pleasant, Barbara. *The Whole Herb: For Cooking, Crafts, Gardening, Health, and Other Joys of Life*. Garden City Park, NY: Square One Publishers, 2004.

Quattrocchi, Umberto. *CRC World Dictionary of Plant Names: Common Names, Scientific Names, Eponyms, Synonyms, and Etymology, Volume 1 A-C*. Boca Raton, FL: CRC Press, LLC, 2000.

Rackwitz, Martin. *Travels to Terra Incognita: The Scottish Highlands and Hebrides in Early Modern Travelers Accounts c. 1600 to 1800*. Munster, Germany: Waxmann Verlag GmbH, 2007.

Radford, Edwin, and Mona A. Radford. *The Encyclopedia of Superstitions.* New York: Philosophical Library, Inc., 2007.

Rich, Vivian A. *Cursing the Basil: And Other Folklore of the Garden.* Victoria, Canada: Horsdal & Schubart Publishers Ltd., 1998.

Ridpath, Ian. *Star Tales.* Cambridge, England: Lutterworth Press, 1988.

Rose, Jeanne. *375 Essential Oils and Hydrosols.* Berkeley, CA: Frog, Ltd., 1999.

Rosean, Lexa. *The Encyclopedia of Magickal Ingredients: A Wiccan Guide to Spellcasting.* New York: Paraview, 2005.

Rosengarten, Jr., Frederic. *The Book of Edible Nuts.* Mineola, NY: Dover Publications, 2004.

Runkel, Sylvan T., and Dean M. Roosa. *Wildflowers and Other Plants of Iowa Wetlands, Second Edition.* Iowa City, IA: Iowa State University Press, 2014.

Sanders, Jack. *Secrets of Wildflowers: A Delightful Feast of Little-Known Facts, Folklore, and History.* Guilford, CT: Globe Pequot Press, 2014.

Shaudys, Phyllis. *The Pleasure of Herbs: A Month-by-Month Guide to Growing, Using, and Enjoying Herbs.* Pownal, VT: Storey Communications, Inc., 1986.

Sifton, David W., ed. *The PDR Family Guide to Natural Medicines and Healing Therapies.* New York: Ballantine Books, 1999.

Small, Ernest, and Paul M. Catling. *Canadian Medicinal Crops.* Ottawa, Canada: National Research Council of Canada, 1999.

———. *Top 100 Food Plants: The World's Most Important Culinary Crops.* Ottawa, Canada: National Research Council of Canada, 2009.

———. *North American Cornucopia: Top 100 Indigenous Food Plants.* Boca Raton, FL: CRC Press, 2014.

Smith, Andrew F. *Food and Drink in American History: A "Full Course" Encyclopedia, Volume 1: A-L.* Santa Barbara, CA: ABC-CLIO, LLC, 2013.

Storl, Wolf D. *The Herbal Lore of Wise Women and Wortcunners: The Healing Power of Medicinal Plants*. Berkeley, CA: North Atlantic Books, 2012.

Sumner, Esther Yu. "A Date is a Date is a Date" *Ancestry Magazine* Vol. 25, No. 2 Mar-Apr 2007. Provo, UT: Ancestry, Inc.

Taylor, Raymond L. *Plants of Colonial Days*. Mineola, NY: Dover Publications, Inc., 1996.

Tenenbaum, Frances, ed. *Taylor's Encyclopedia of Garden Plants*. New York: Houghton Mifflin Company, 2003.

Thiselton-Dyer, T. F. *The Folk-Lore of Plants*. New York: D. Appleton and Company, 1889.

Tucker, Arthur O., and Thomas DeBaggio. *The Encyclopedia of Herbs: A Comprehensive Reference to Herbs of Flavor and Fragrance*. Portland, OR: Timber Press, Inc., 2009.

Vickery, Roy, ed. *Oxford Dictionary of Plant-Lore*. Oxford: Oxford University Press, 1997.

Watts, D. C. *Dictionary of Plant Lore*. Burlington, MA: Academic Press, 2007.

Wheelwright, Edith Grey. *Medicinal Plants and Their History*. New York: Dover Publications, Inc. 1974.

White, Carolyn. *A History of Irish Fairies*. Dublin, Ireland: Mercier Press, 2001.

Whitehurst, Tess. *The Magic of Flowers: A Guide to Their Metaphysical Uses & Properties*. Woodbury, MN: Llewellyn Publications, 2013.

Wilson, Roberta. *Aromatherapy: Essential Oils for Vibrant Health and Beauty*. New York: Penguin Putnam, Inc., 2002.

Wood, Matthew. *The Book of Herbal Wisdom: Using Plants as Medicine*. Berkeley, CA: North Atlantic Books, 1997.

———. *The Earthwise Herbal: A Complete Guide to Old World Medicinal Plants*. Berkeley, CA: North Atlantic Books, 2009.

Wright, Walter P. *An Encyclopaedia of Gardening*. Bremen, Germany: Salzwasser-Verlag, 2010.

Zolar. *Zolar's Encyclopedia and Dictionary of Dreams*. New York: Fireside, 1992.

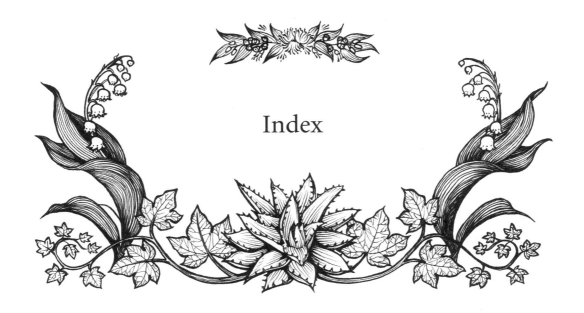

# Index

violet
  *candied,* 61
  *plant,* 55–58, 61, 67, 72, 86, 96
Vulcan, 24, 102, 196

# W

Walpurgis, 67

wassail, 21

wild carrot, 171

wild ginger, 185

willow, 65–67, 169, 215, 218–220

witch hazel, 24, 25, 215

witches' bells, 102

witches' briar, 114

witches' candle, 106

wolf's bane, 139

wolfberry, 43, 44, 215, 218–220

wolfsbane, 7, 132, 139, 205, 218, 220

woodbine, 140

woody nightshade, 166

wormwood, 121, 122

woundwort, 154

# Y

yarrow, 7, 8, 92, 99, 215, 217–221

yew, 181, 182, 215, 217, 218, 220

Yggdrasil, 37

yucca, 60, 61, 215, 219, 220

Yule, 19, 22, 115, 173, 175, 176, 182, 187, 188, 190, 194, 197, 199

# Z

Zeus, 40, 57, 67, 70, 71, 85, 98, 105, 123, 146, 151, 194, 201

## To Write to the Author

If you wish to contact the author or would like more information about this book, please write to the author in care of Llewellyn Worldwide, Ltd. and we will forward your request. The authors and publisher appreciate hearing from you and learning of your enjoyment of this book and how it has helped you. Llewellyn Worldwide, Ltd. cannot guarantee that every letter written to the author can be answered, but all will be forwarded. Please write to:

Sandra Kynes
℅ Llewellyn Worldwide
2143 Wooddale Drive
Woodbury, MN 55125-2989

Please enclose a self-addressed stamped envelope for reply,
or $1.00 to cover costs. If outside the USA,
enclose an international postal reply coupon.